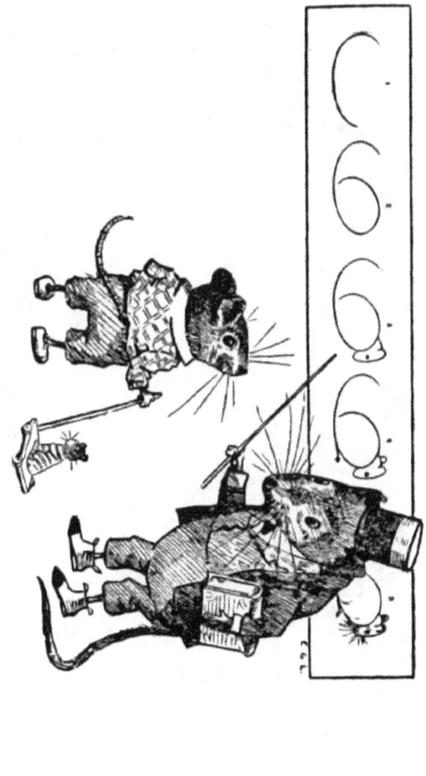

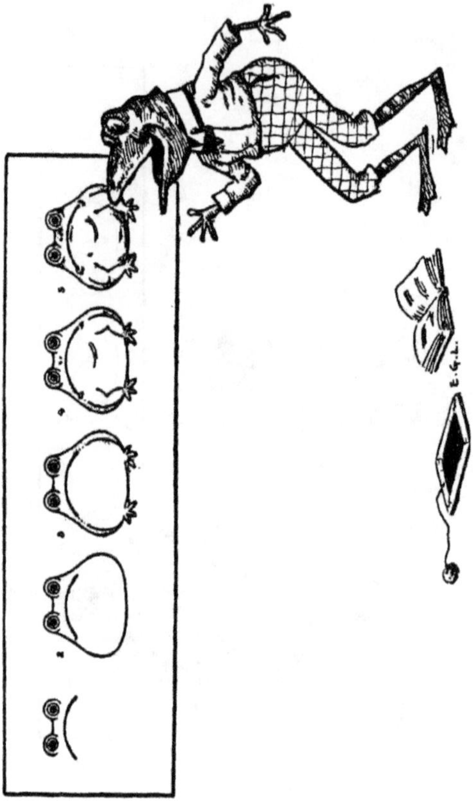

ISBN-13: 978-1519615510
ISBN-10: 1519615515

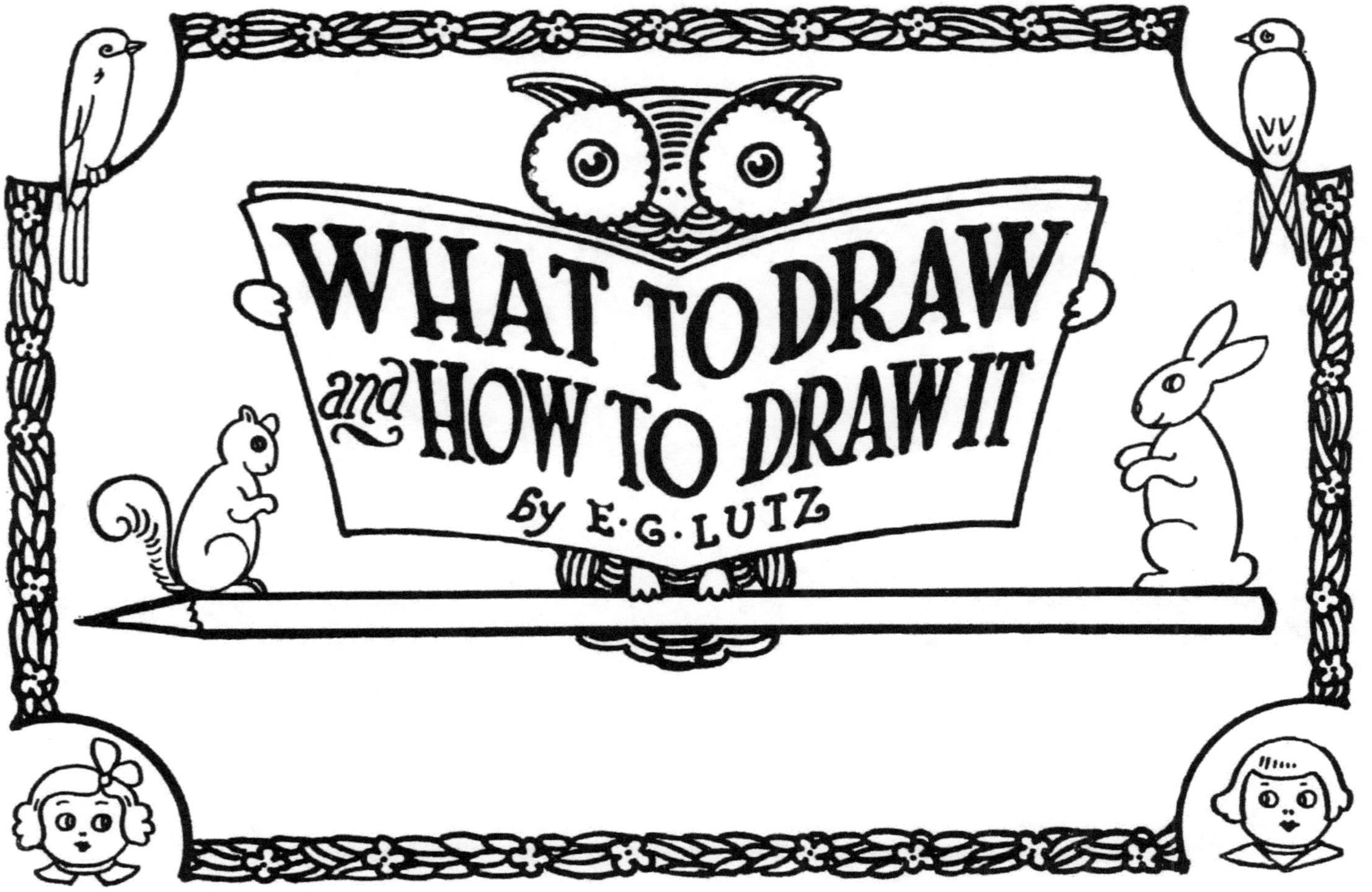
WHAT TO DRAW
and HOW TO DRAW IT
by E·G·LUTZ

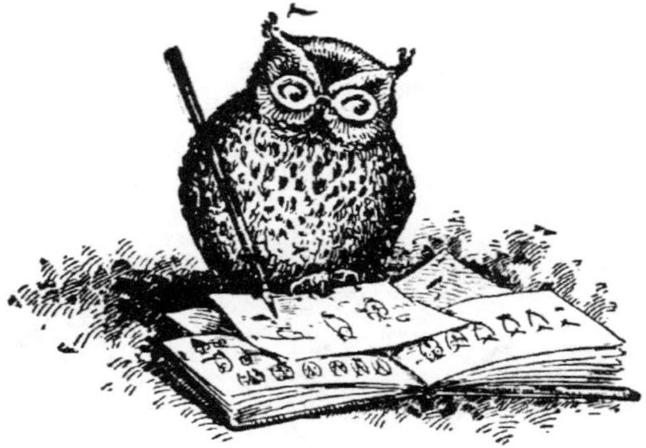

INSTRUCTIONS

In drawing from this book, copy the last diagram, or finished picture, of the particular series before you.

The other diagrams—beginning with number one, then number two, and so on—show how to go on with your drawing. They give the order in which to make the various strokes of the pencil that together form the completed picture. The dotted lines indicate where light lines are drawn that help in construction—that is; getting proportions correctly, outlining the general form, or marking details in their proper places. Do not press hard on the pencil in making these construction lines, then they can be erased afterwards.

Use pencil compasses for the circles, or mark them off with buttons or disks.

To Draw a Five-Pointed Star

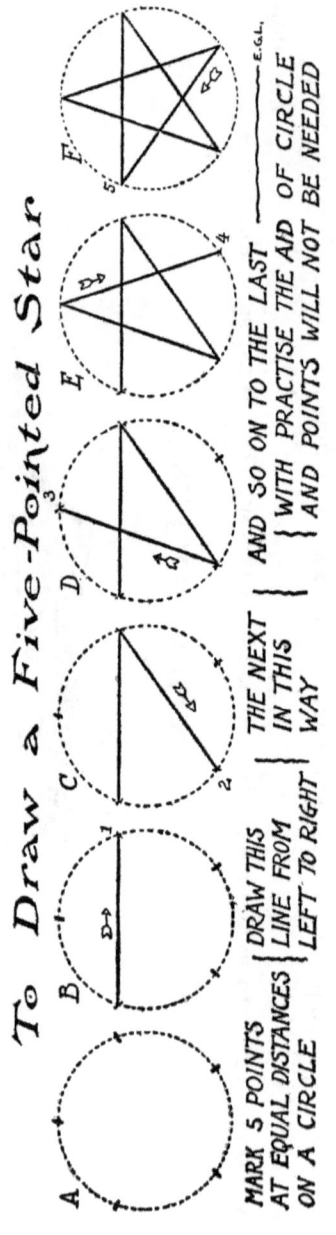

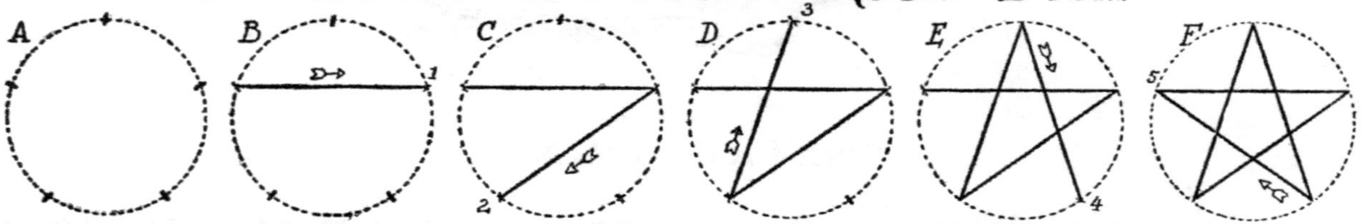

MARK 5 POINTS AT EQUAL DISTANCES ON A CIRCLE | DRAW THIS LINE FROM LEFT TO RIGHT | THE NEXT IN THIS WAY | AND SO ON TO THE LAST

WITH PRACTISE THE AID OF CIRCLE AND POINTS WILL NOT BE NEEDED

E.G.L.

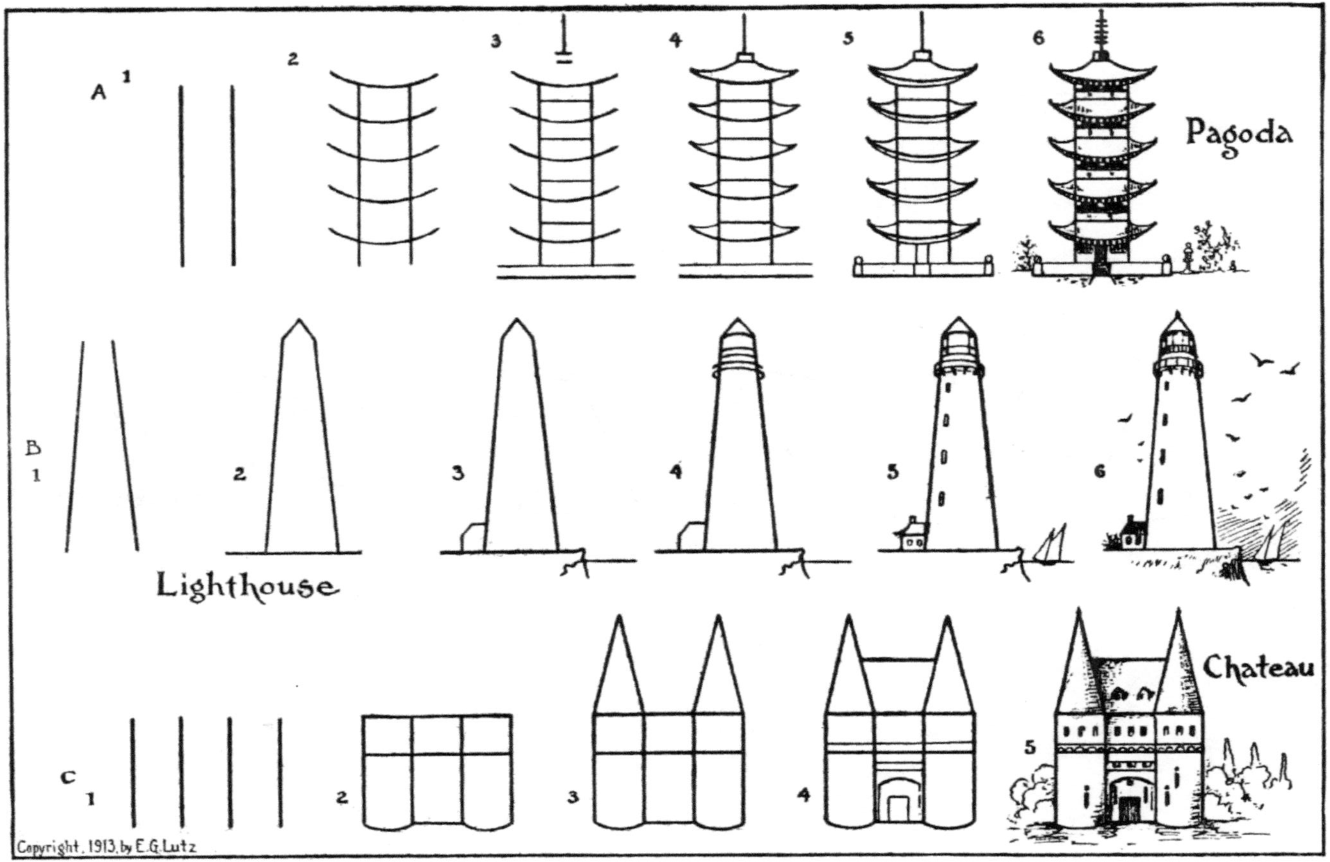
A 1
2
3
4
5
6
Pagoda
B 1
2
3
4
5
6
Lighthouse
C 1
2
3
4
5
Chateau
Copyright, 1913, by E.G. Lutz

Tent

1
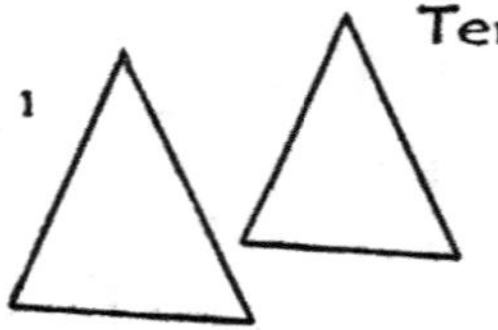

2
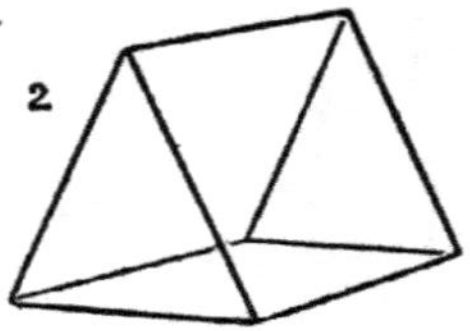

3
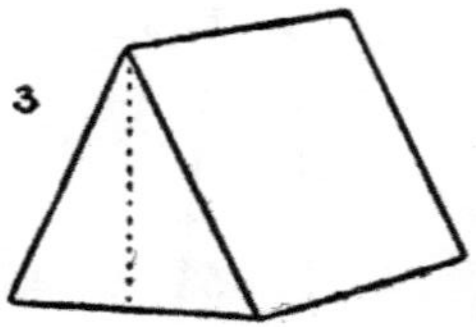

4
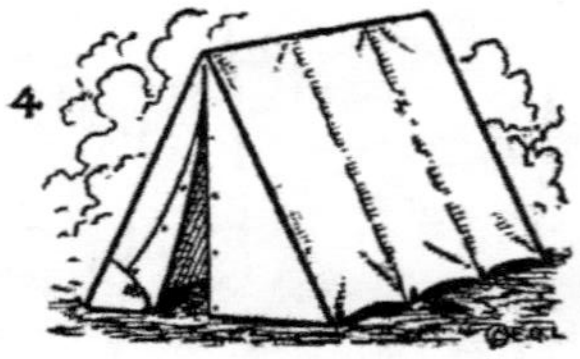

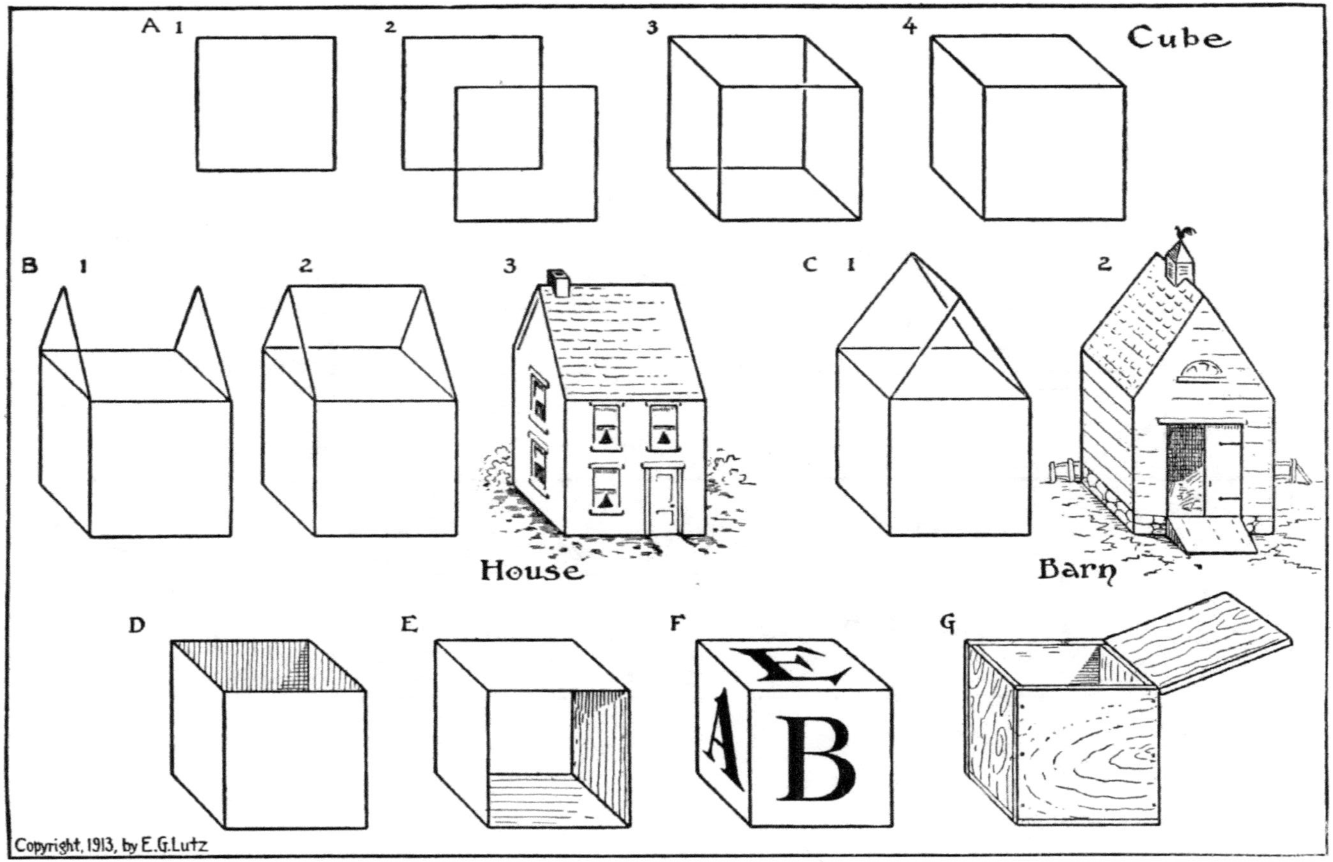
Cube
A 1
2
3
4
B 1
2
3
House
C 1
2
Barn
D
E
F
G
Copyright, 1913, by E.G.Lutz

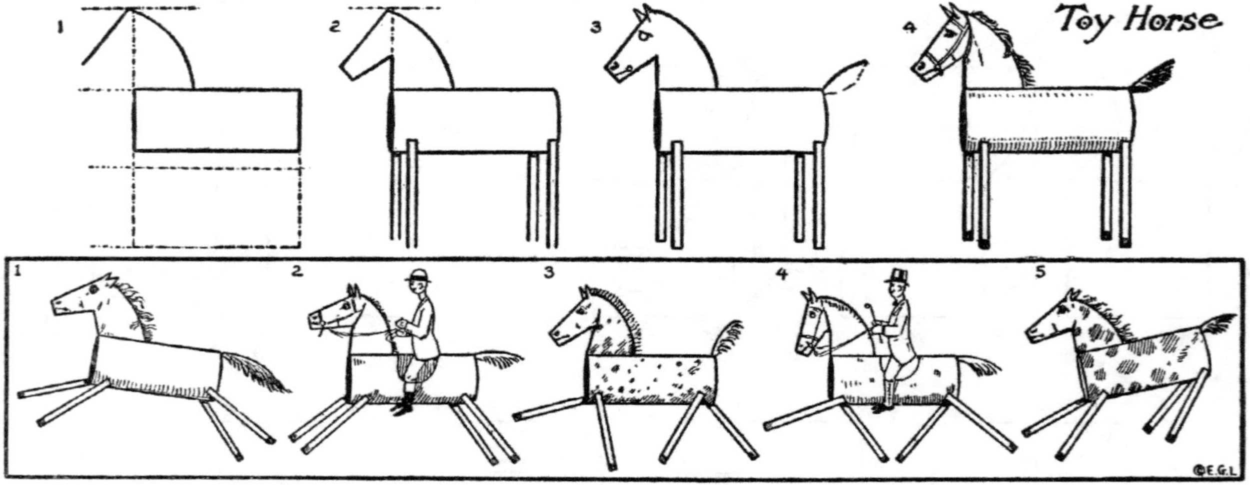
Toy Horse
1
2
3
4
1
2
3
4
5
©E.G.L

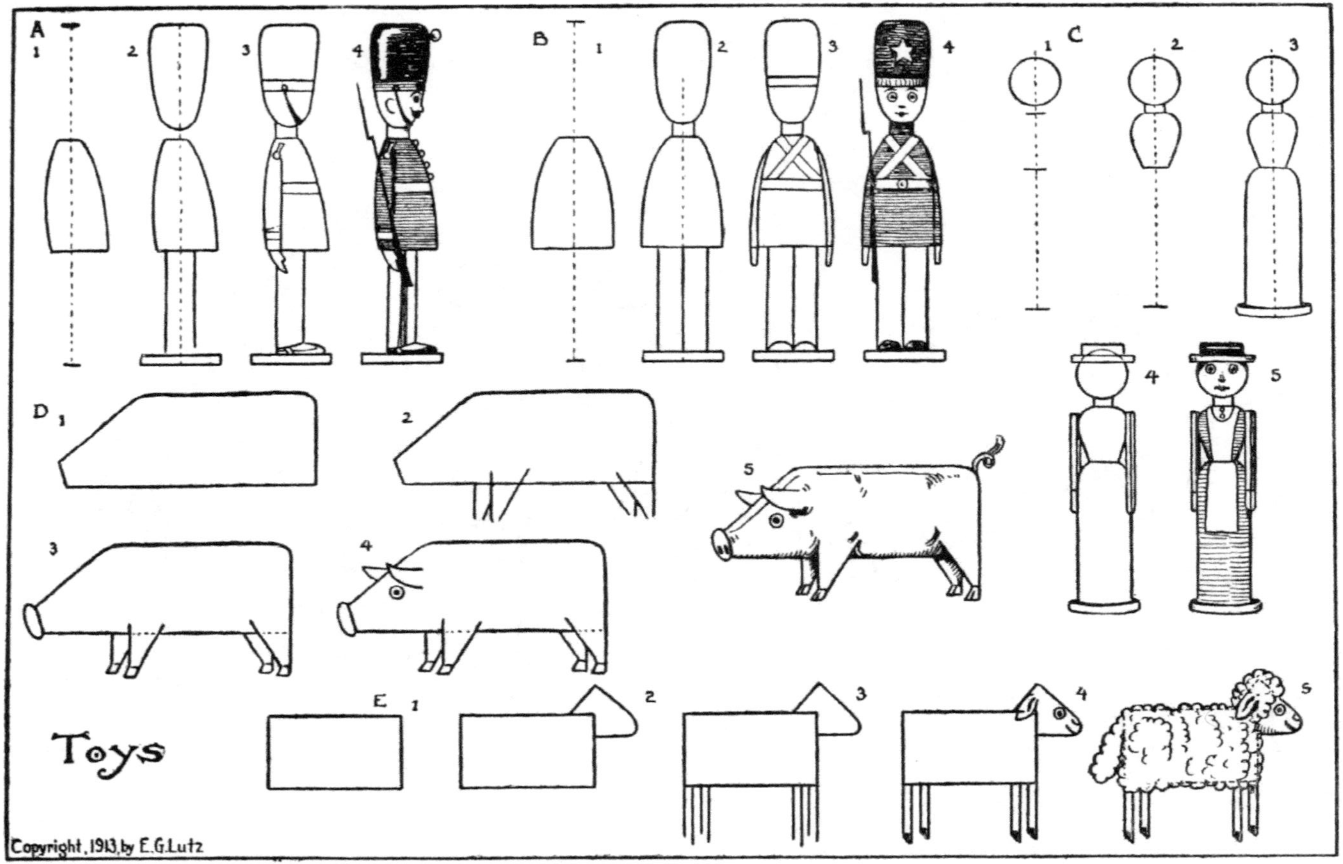
A
1
2
3
4
B
1
2
3
4
C
1
2
3
4
5
D
1
2
3
4
5
E
1
2
3
4
5
Toys
Copyright, 1913, by E.G.Lutz

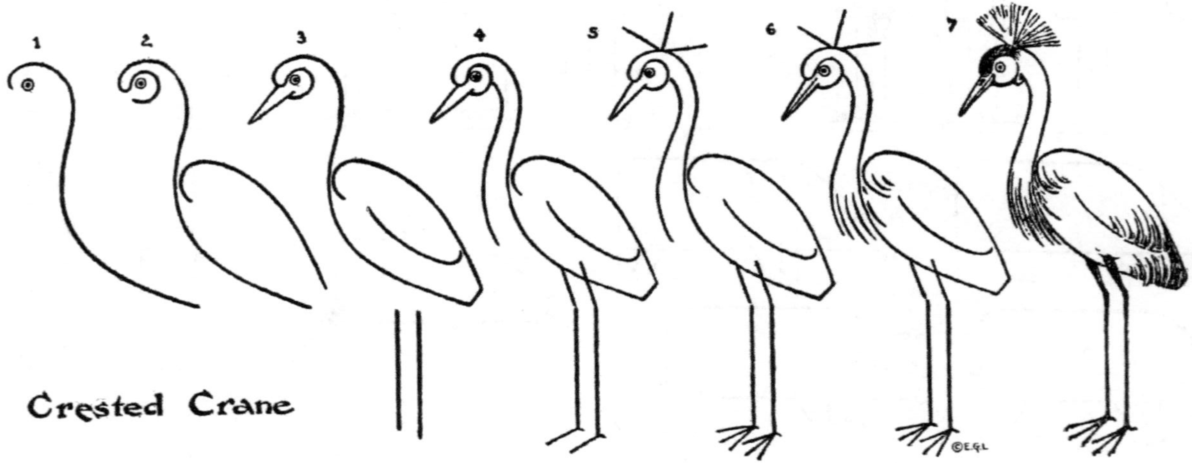

Crested Crane

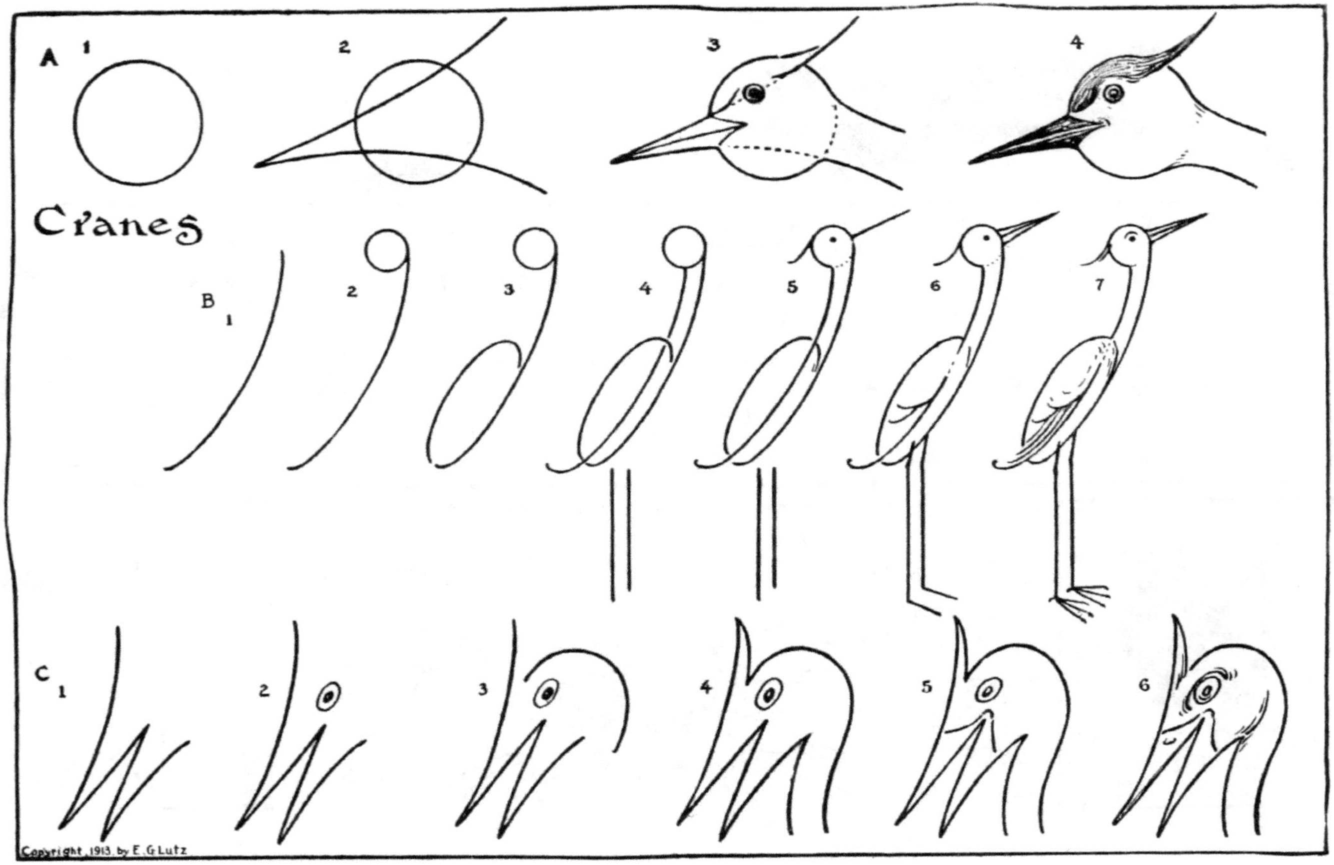
Cranes
A
1
2
3
4
B
1
2
3
4
5
6
7
C
1
2
3
4
5
6
Copyright, 1913, by E. G. Lutz

Cat

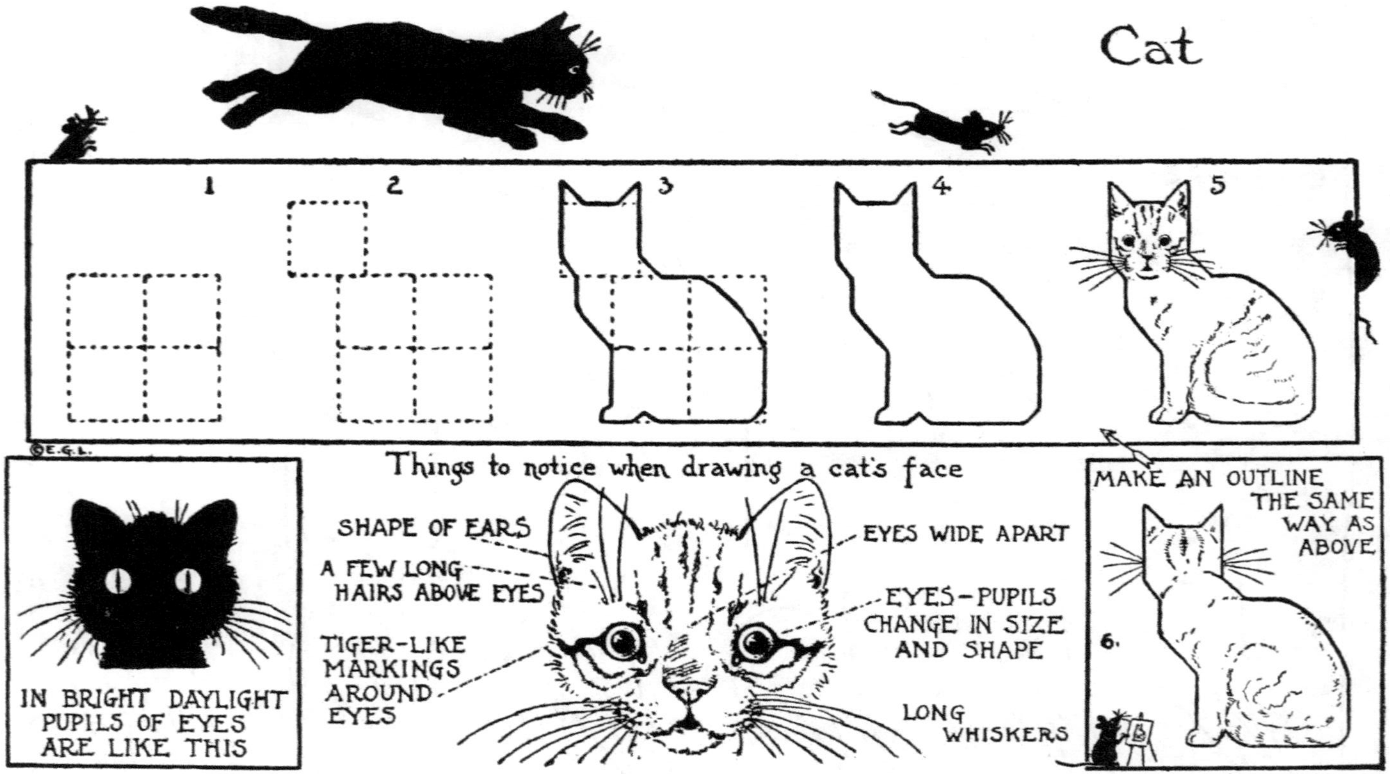

1
2
3
4
5
©E.G.L.
Things to notice when drawing a cat's face
IN BRIGHT DAYLIGHT PUPILS OF EYES ARE LIKE THIS
SHAPE OF EARS
A FEW LONG HAIRS ABOVE EYES
TIGER-LIKE MARKINGS AROUND EYES
EYES WIDE APART
EYES–PUPILS CHANGE IN SIZE AND SHAPE
LONG WHISKERS
MAKE AN OUTLINE THE SAME WAY AS ABOVE
6.

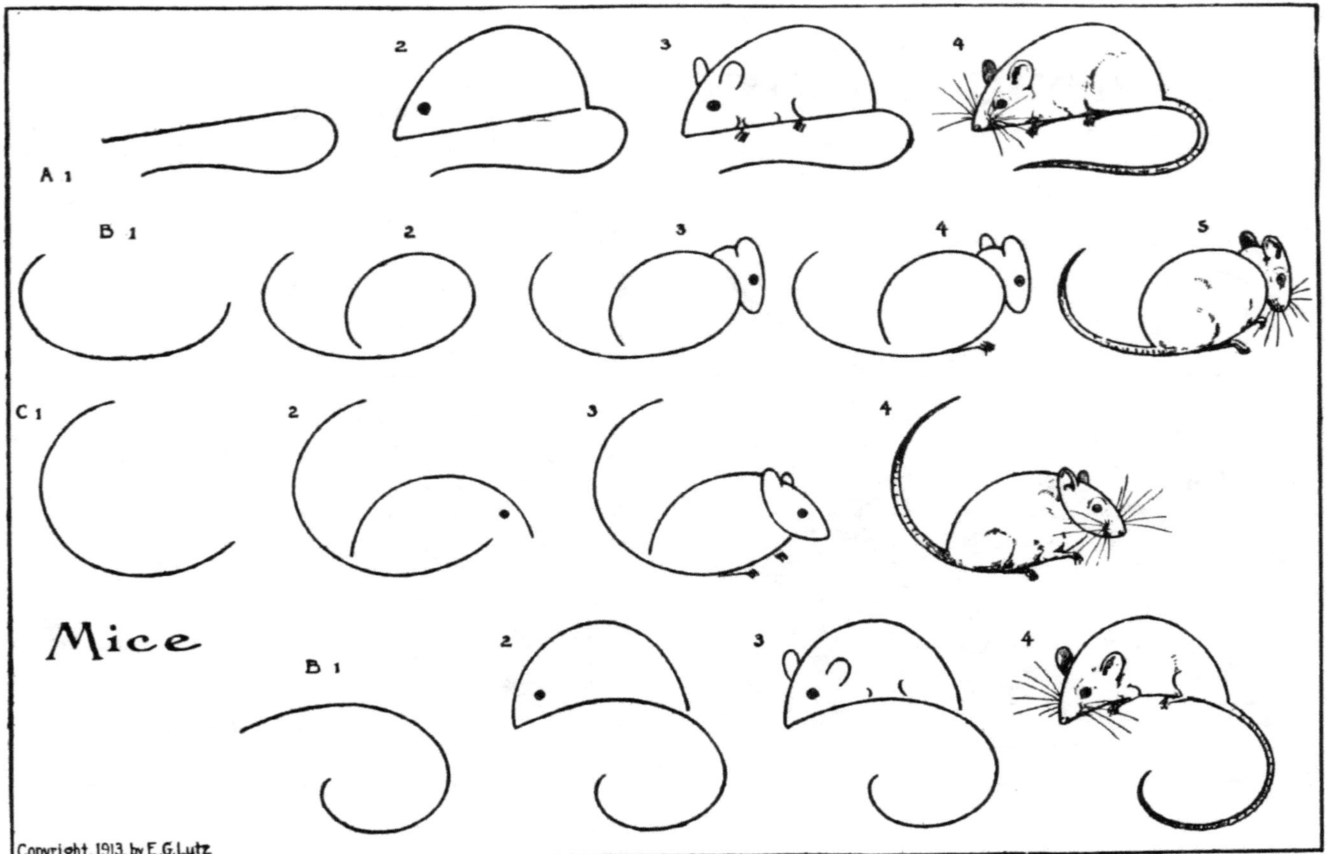

A 1
2
3
4
B 1
2
3
4
5
C 1
2
3
4
Mice
B 1
2
3
4

CURIOUS FISHES

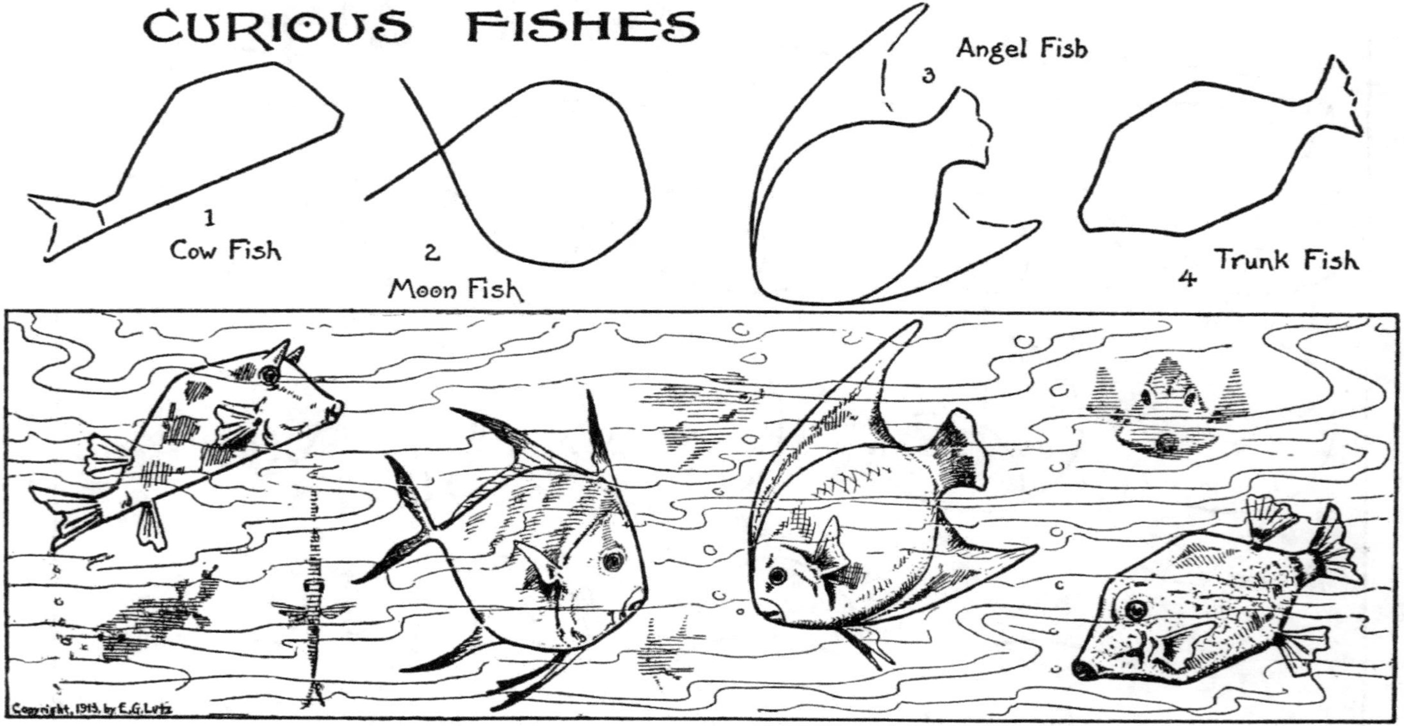
1
Cow Fish
2
Moon Fish
3
Angel Fisb
4
Trunk Fish
Copyright, 1913, by E.G. Lutz

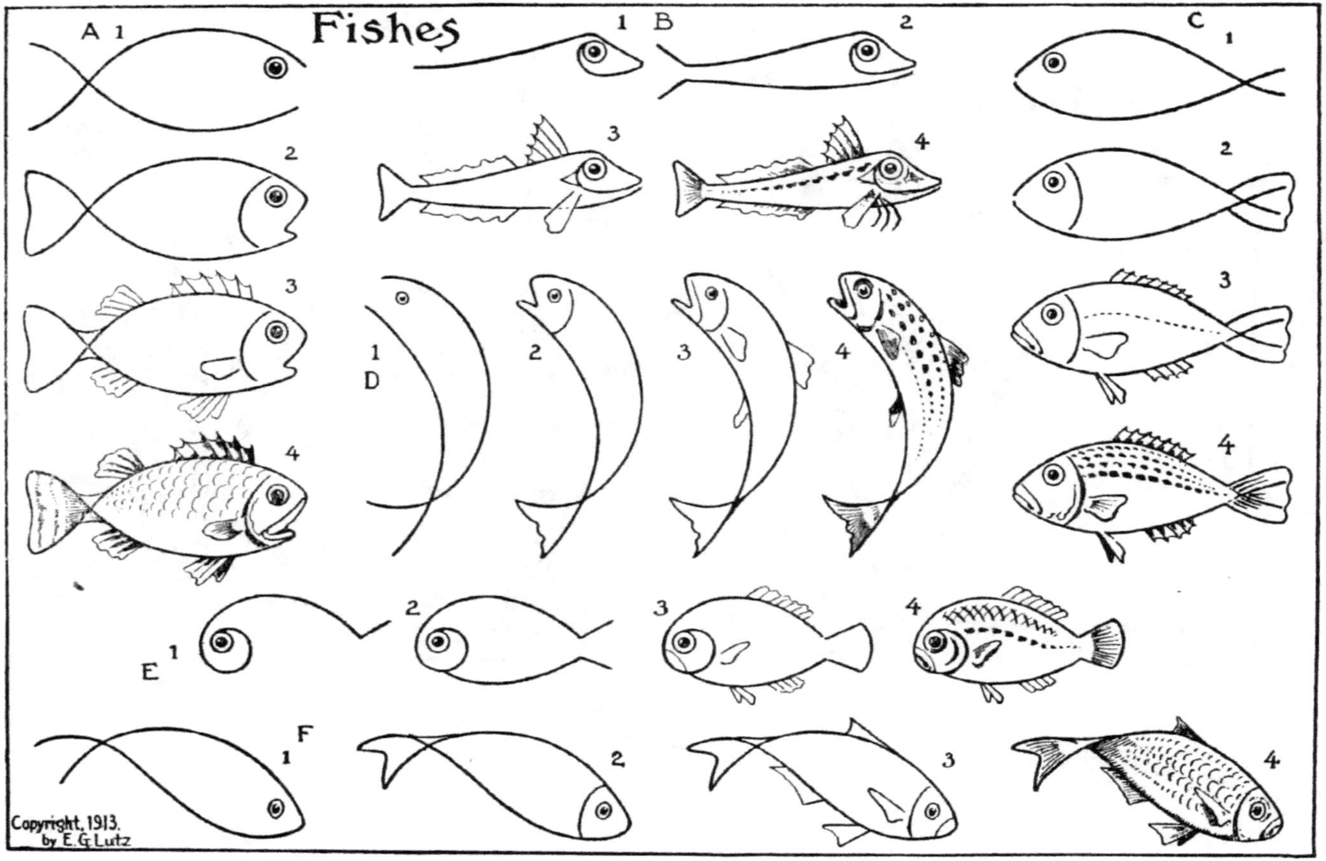
Fishes
A 1
2
3
4
1 B
2
3
4
C 1
2
3
4
1 D
2
3
4
E 1
2
3
4
1 F
2
3
4
Copyright, 1913, by E. G. Lutz

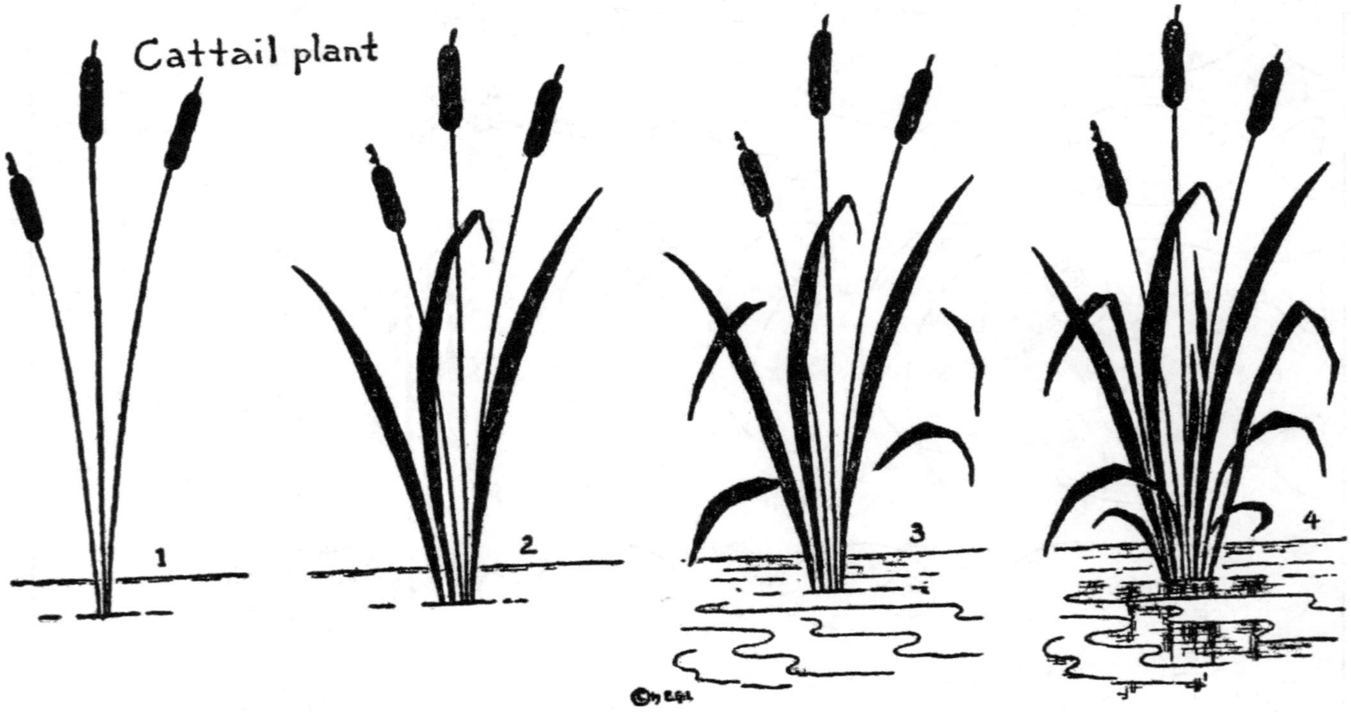
Cattail plant
1
2
3
4

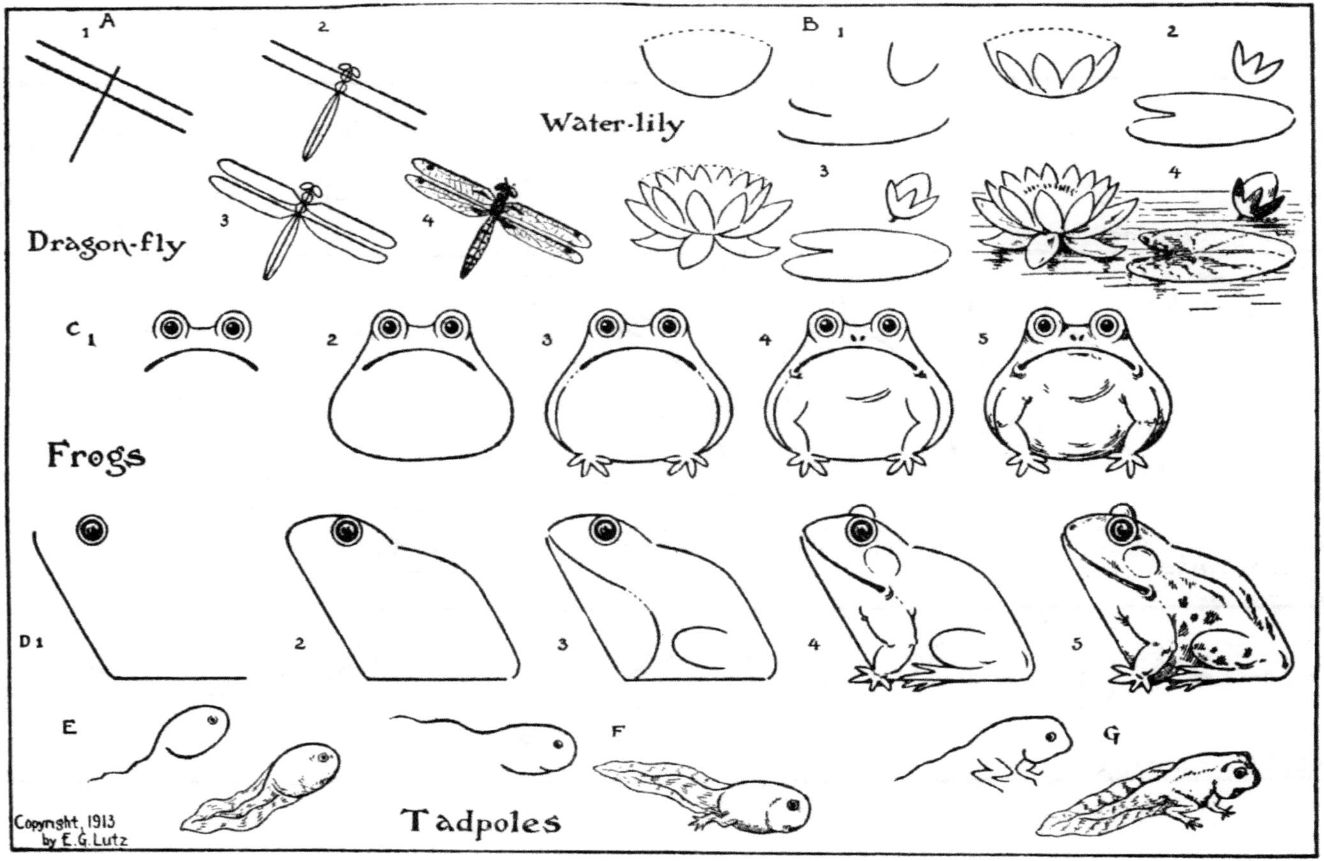
Dragon-fly
Water-lily
Frogs
Tadpoles
Copyright, 1913
by E. G. Lutz

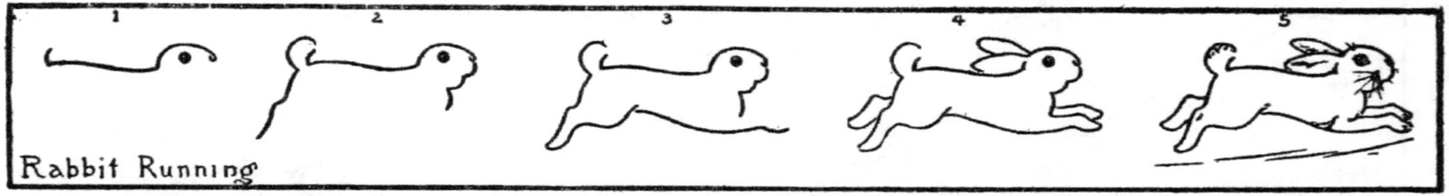
1
2
3
4
5
Rabbit Running

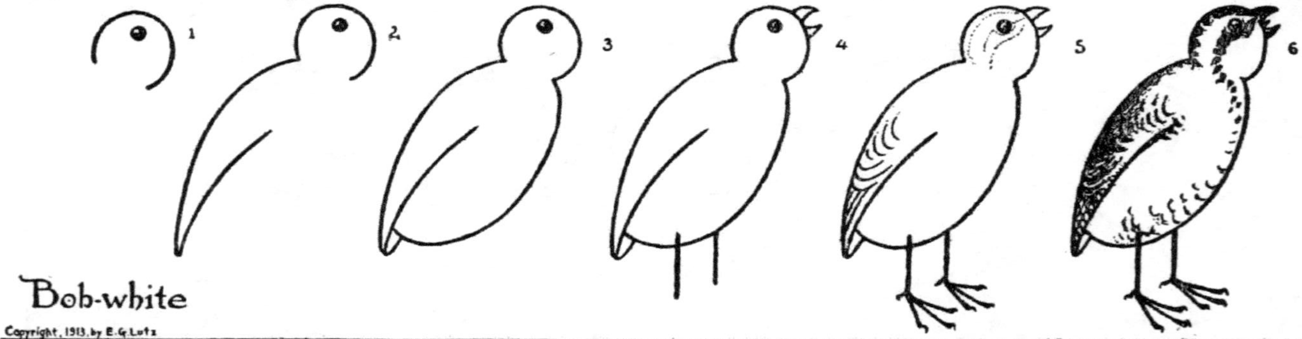
1
2
3
4
5
6
Bob-white
Copyright, 1913, by E. G. Lutz

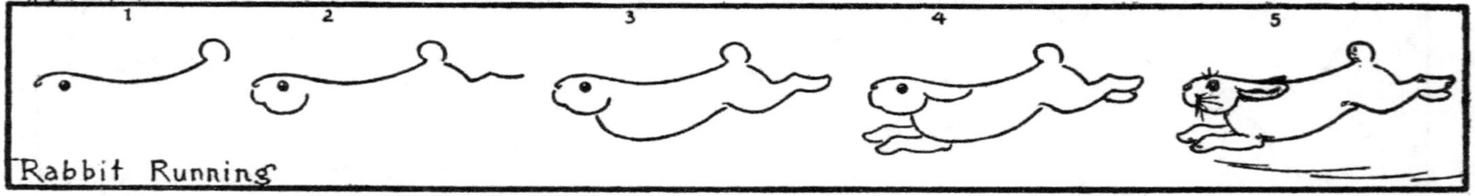
1
2
3
4
5
Rabbit Running

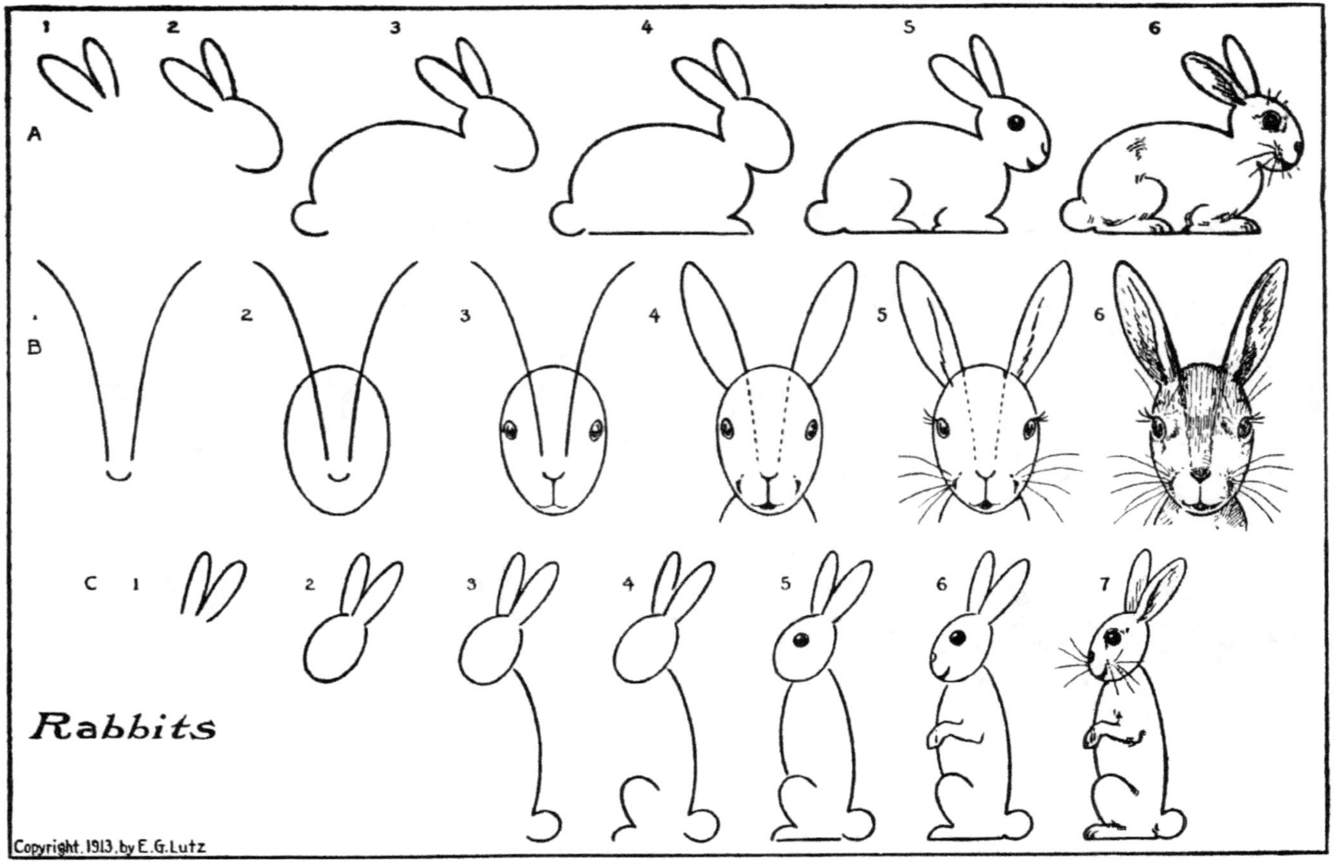
1
2
3
4
5
6
A
B
2
3
4
5
6
C
1
2
3
4
5
6
7
Rabbits
Copyright. 1913. by E.G.Lutz

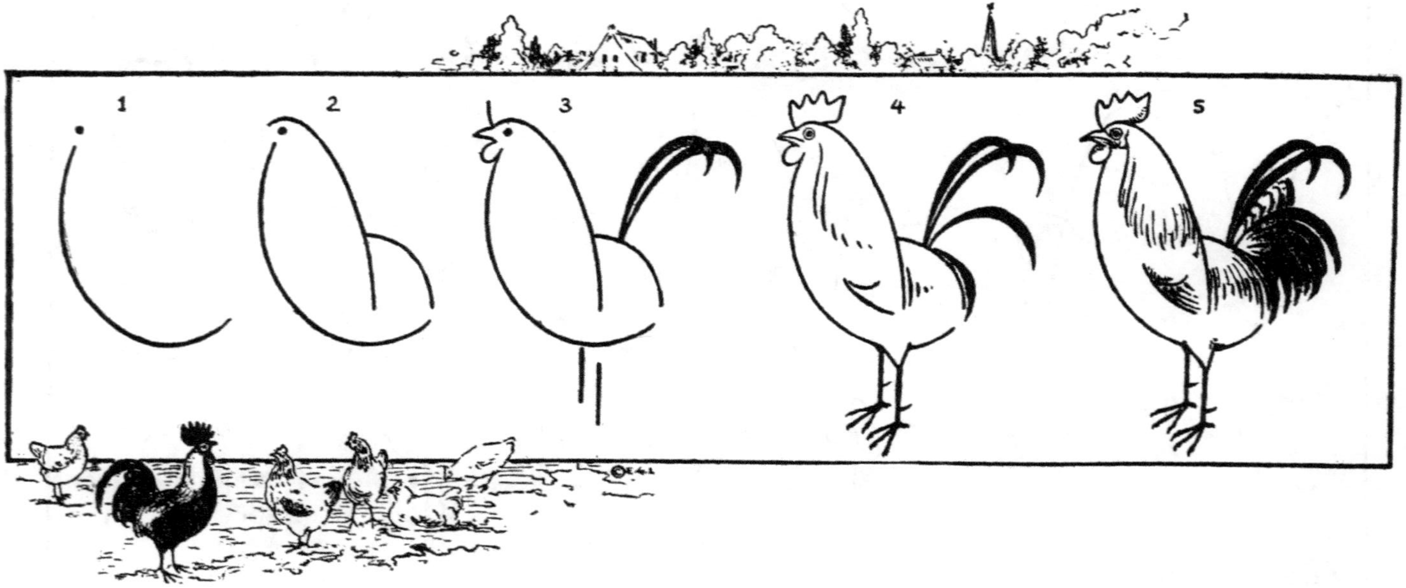
1
2
3
4
5

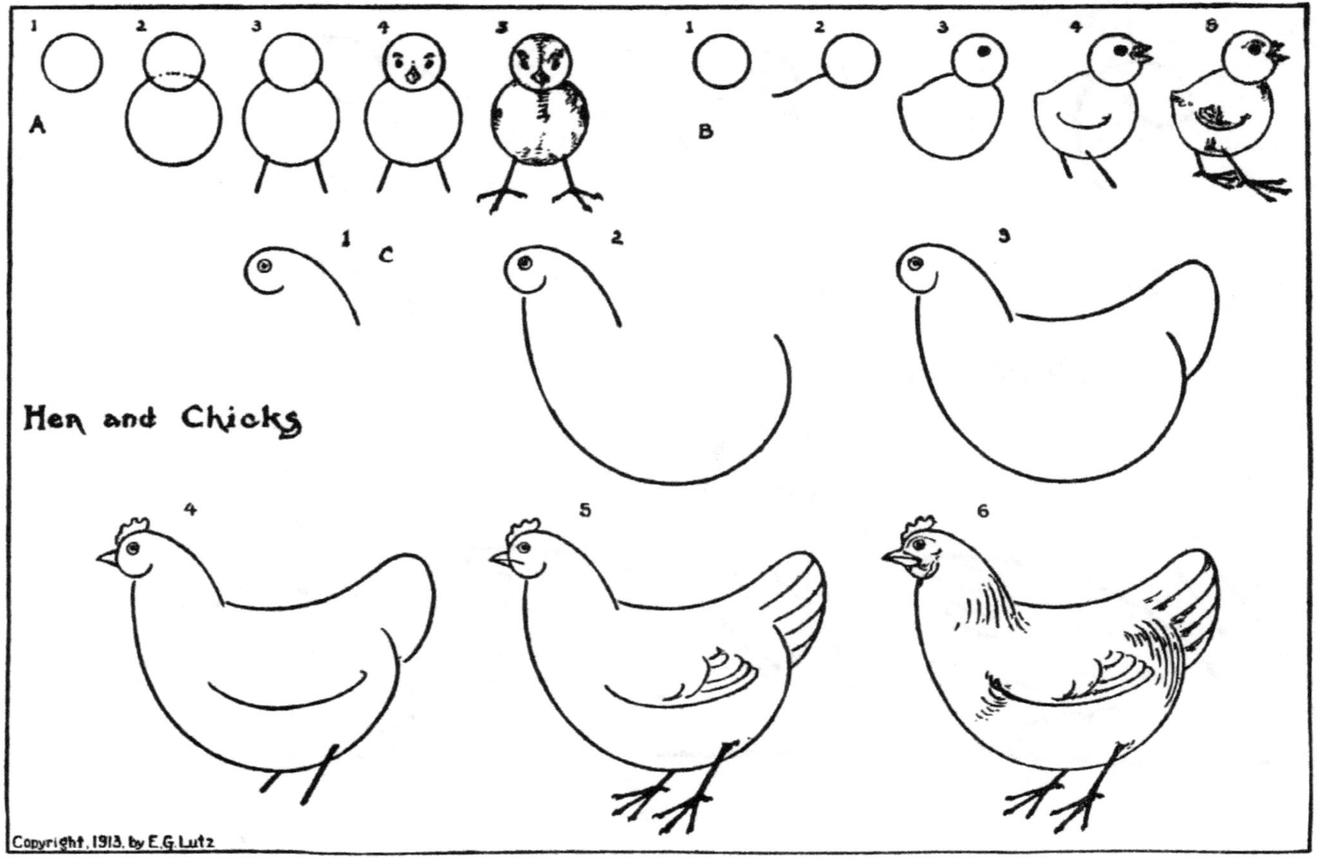
1
2
3
4
5
A
1
2
3
4
5
B
1
C
2
3
Hen and Chicks
4
5
6
Copyright, 1913, by E.G. Lutz

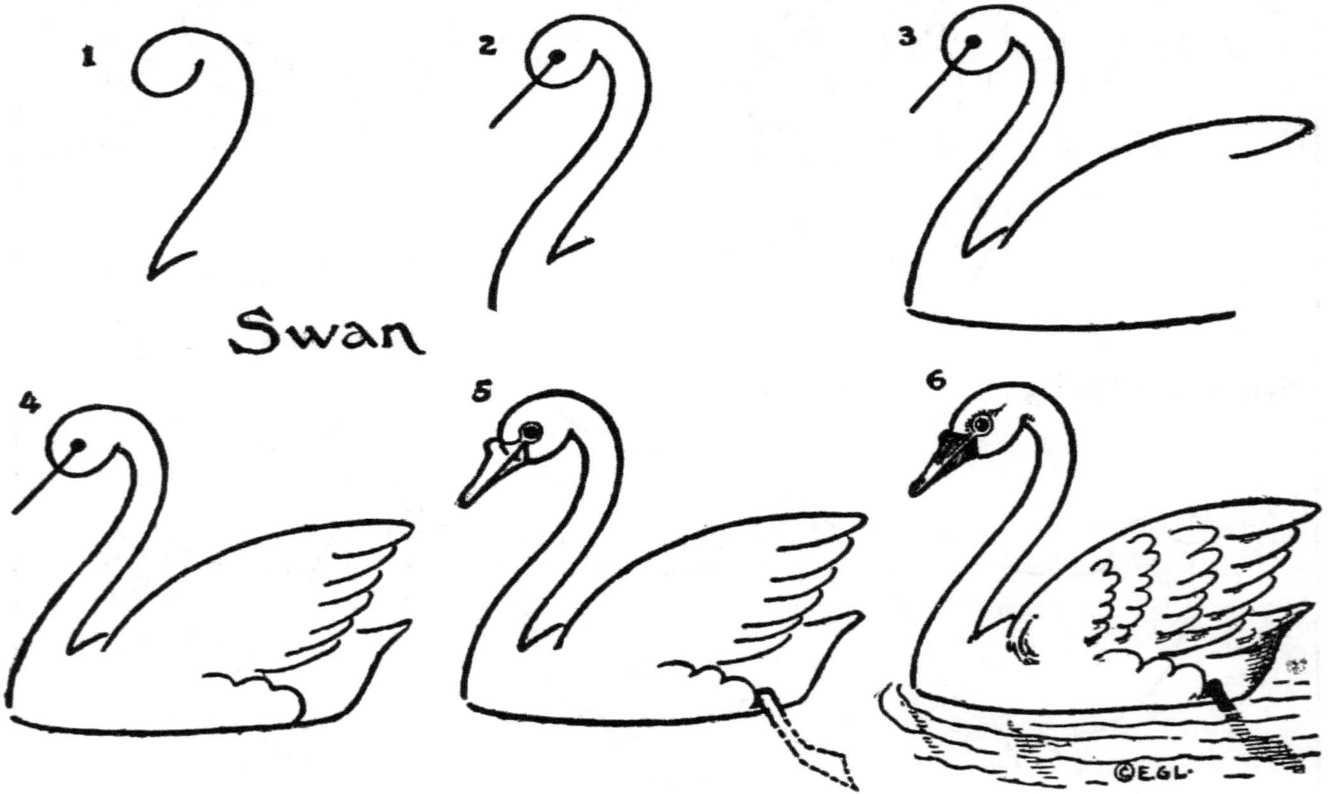
1
2
3
Swan
4
5
6
©E.G.L.

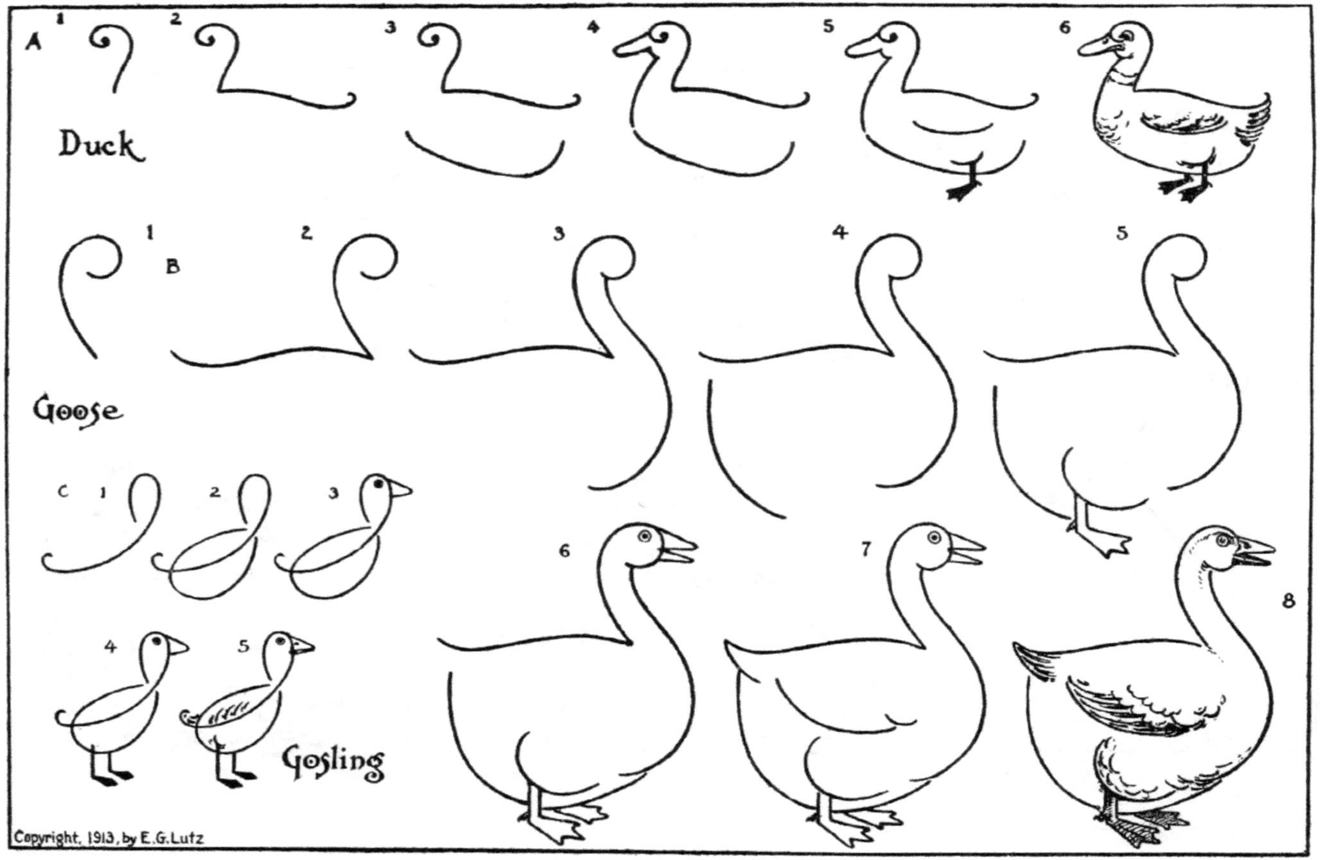
A
1
2
3
4
5
6
Duck
1
B
2
3
4
5
Goose
C
1
2
3
4
5
Gosling
6
7
8
Copyright, 1913, by E.G.Lutz

Cow

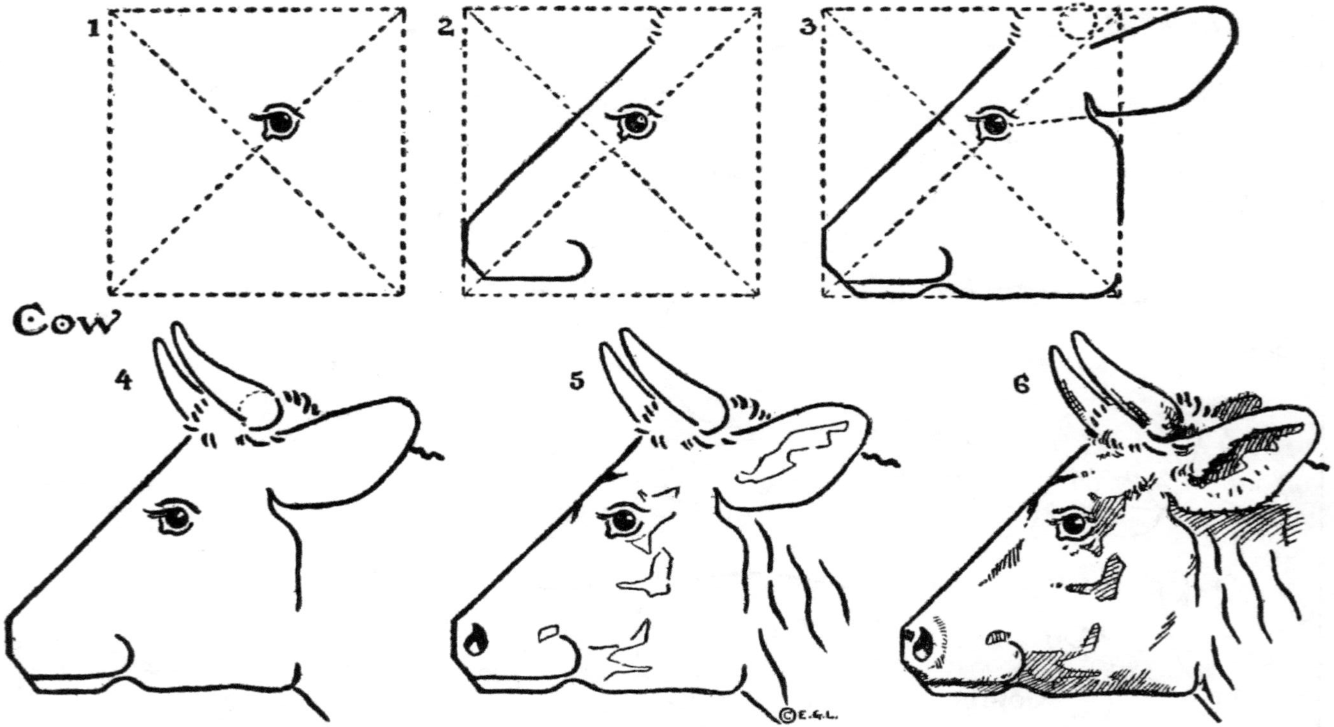

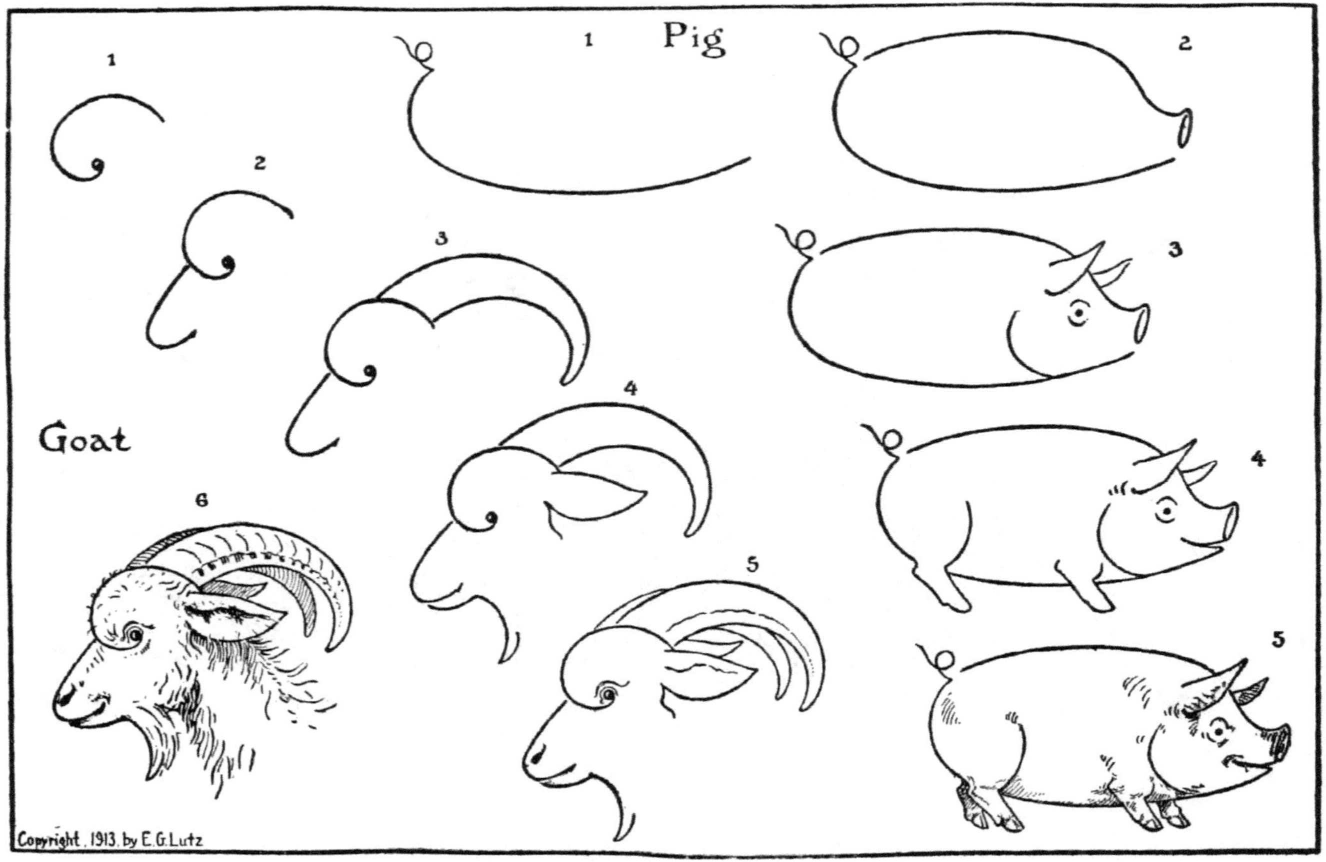
Pig
1
2
3
4
5
Goat
1
2
3
4
5
6
Copyright, 1913, by E. G. Lutz

Bulldog

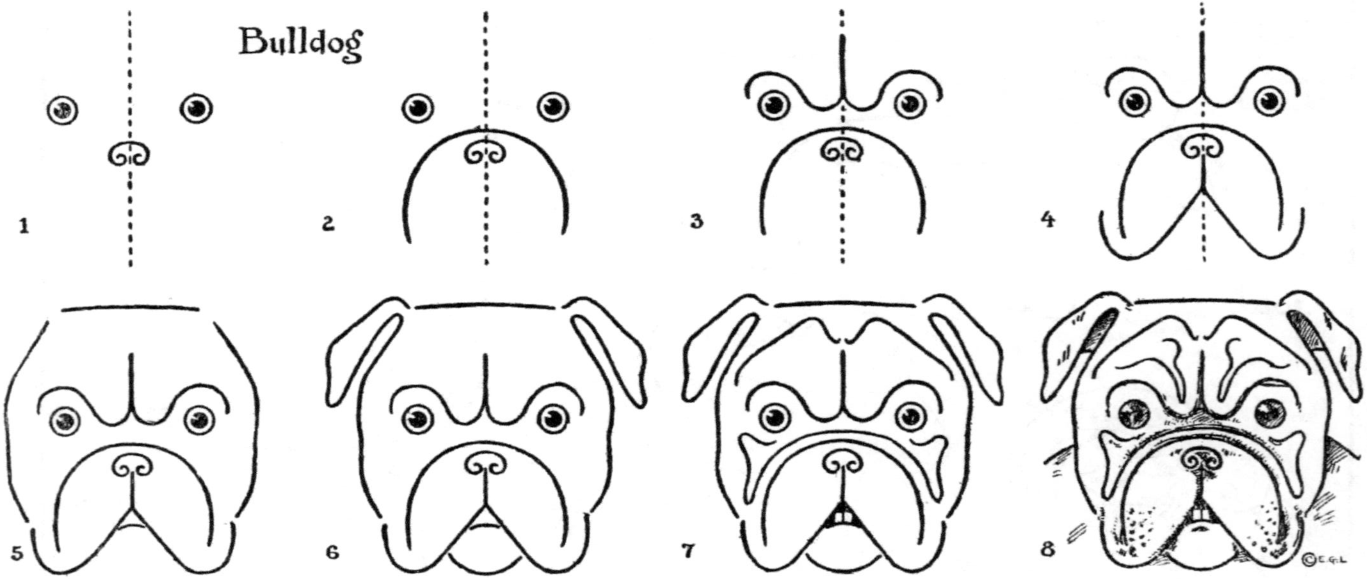

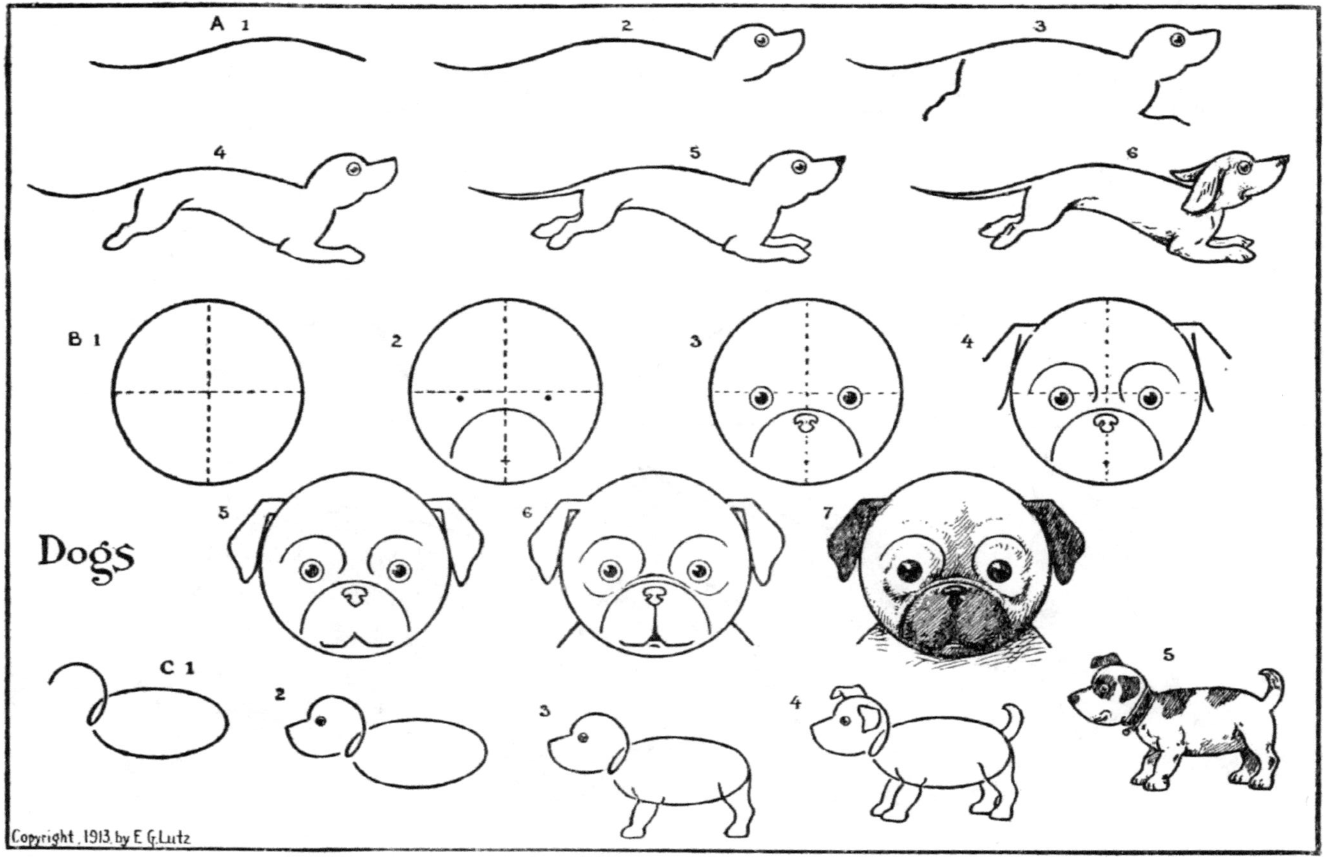
A 1
2
3
4
5
6
B 1
2
3
4
5
6
7
Dogs
C 1
2
3
4
5
Copyright, 1913, by E. G. Lutz

Horse

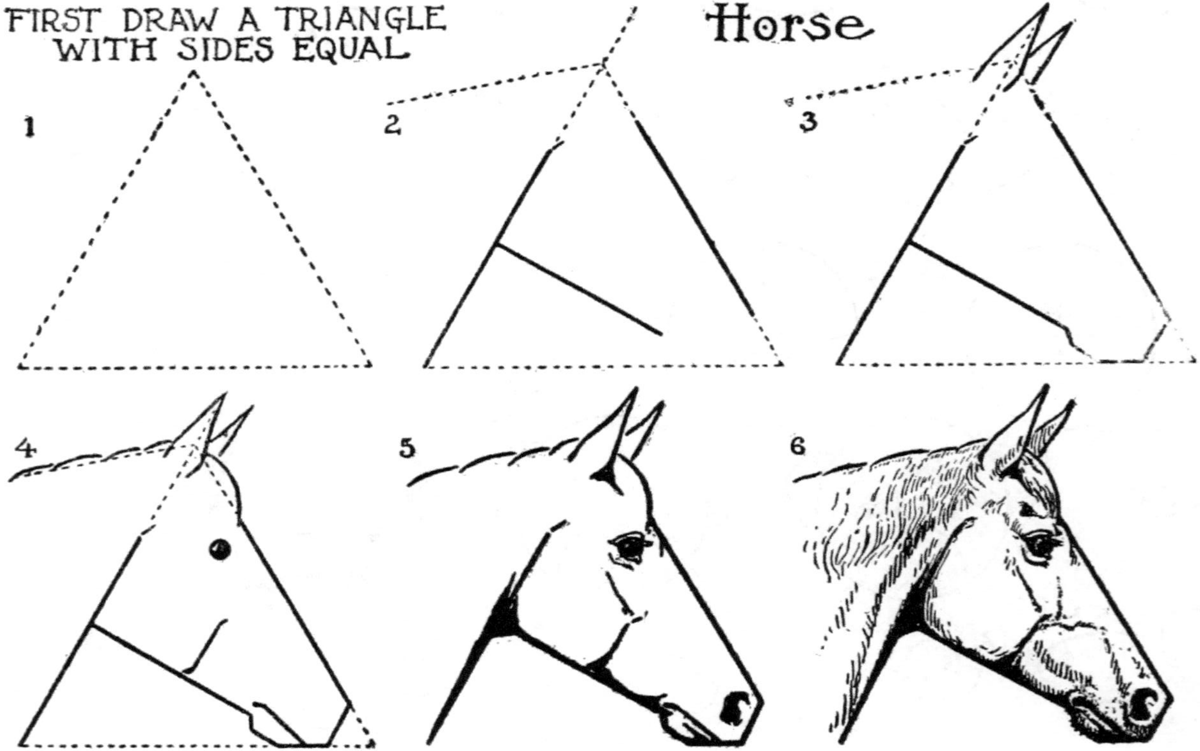
FIRST DRAW A TRIANGLE
WITH SIDES EQUAL
1
2
3
4
5
6

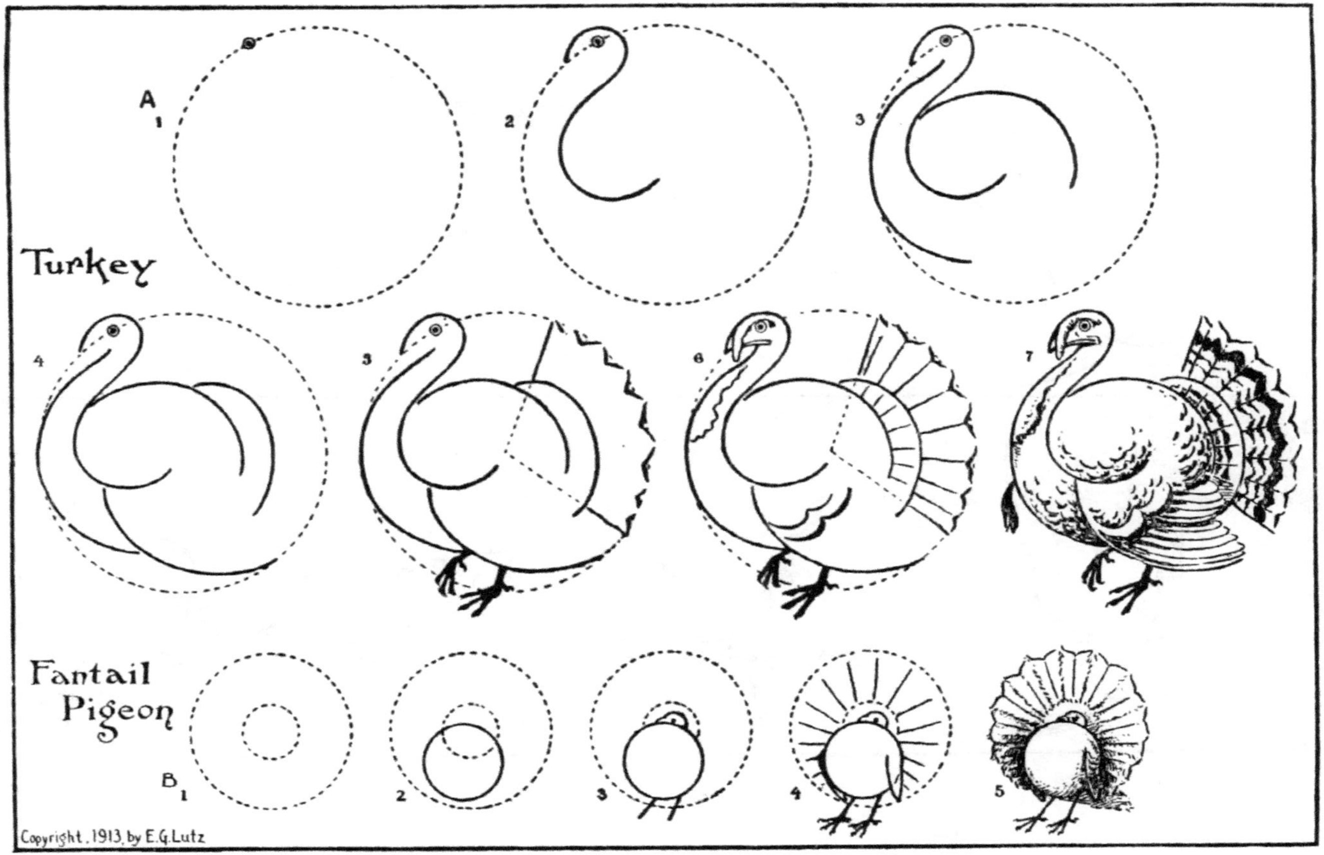
Turkey
A 1
2
3
4
5
6
7
Fantail Pigeon
B 1
2
3
4
5
Copyright, 1913, by E.G.Lutz

Humming-Birds

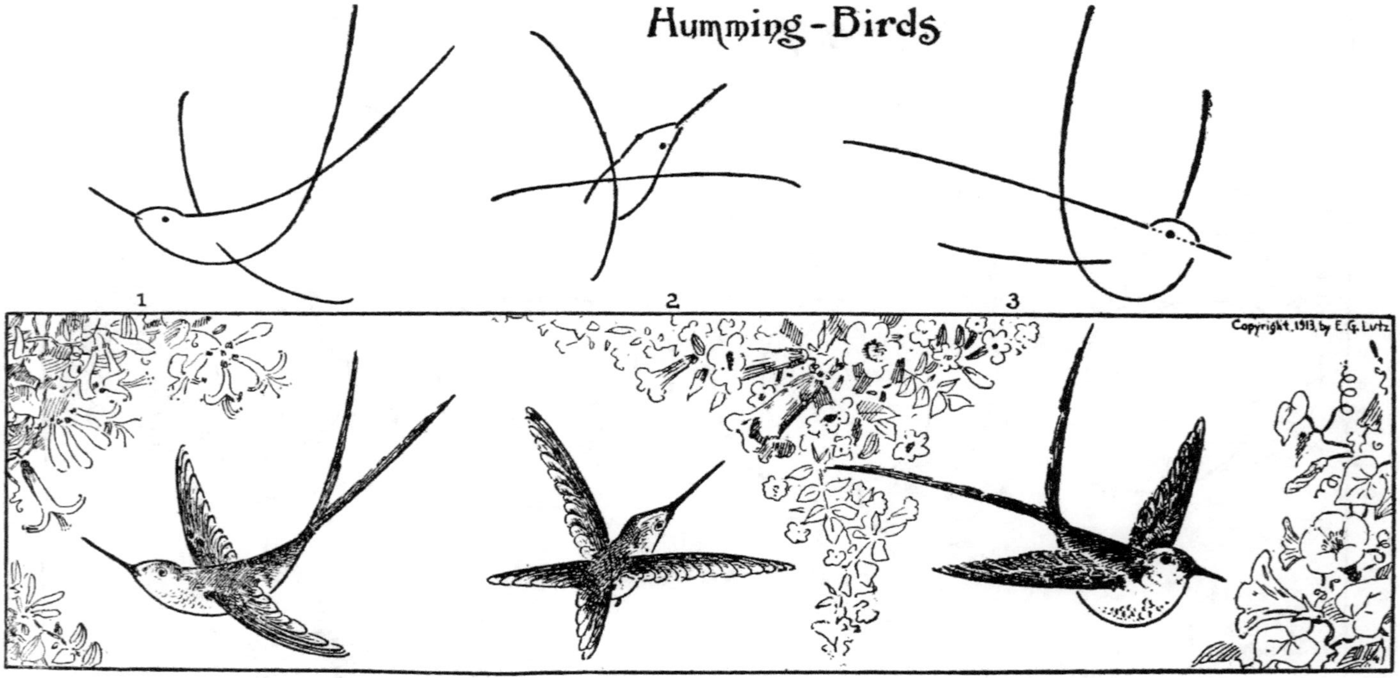

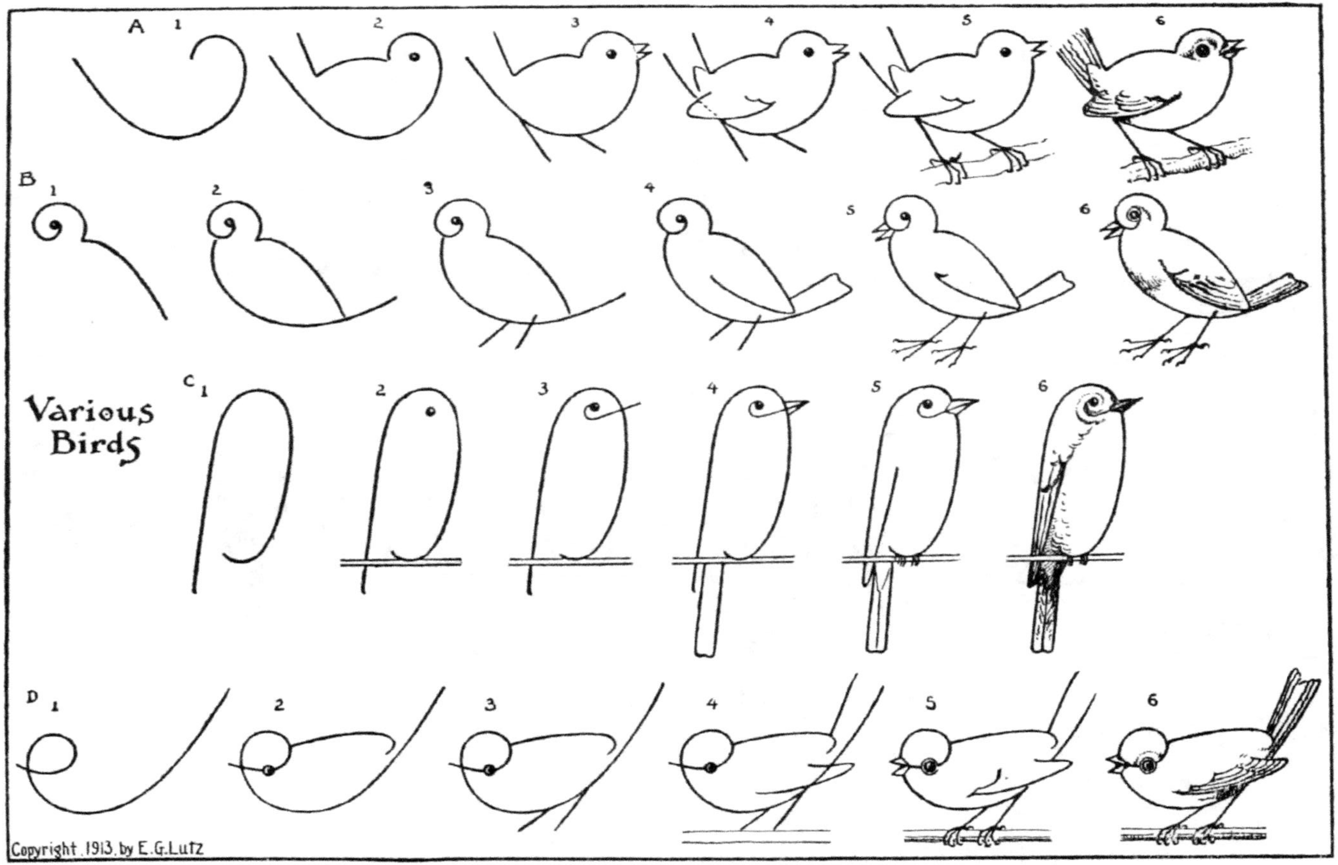

Various Birds
A 1 2 3 4 5 6
B 1 2 3 4 5 6
C 1 2 3 4 5 6
D 1 2 3 4 5 6
Copyright. 1913. by E.G.Lutz

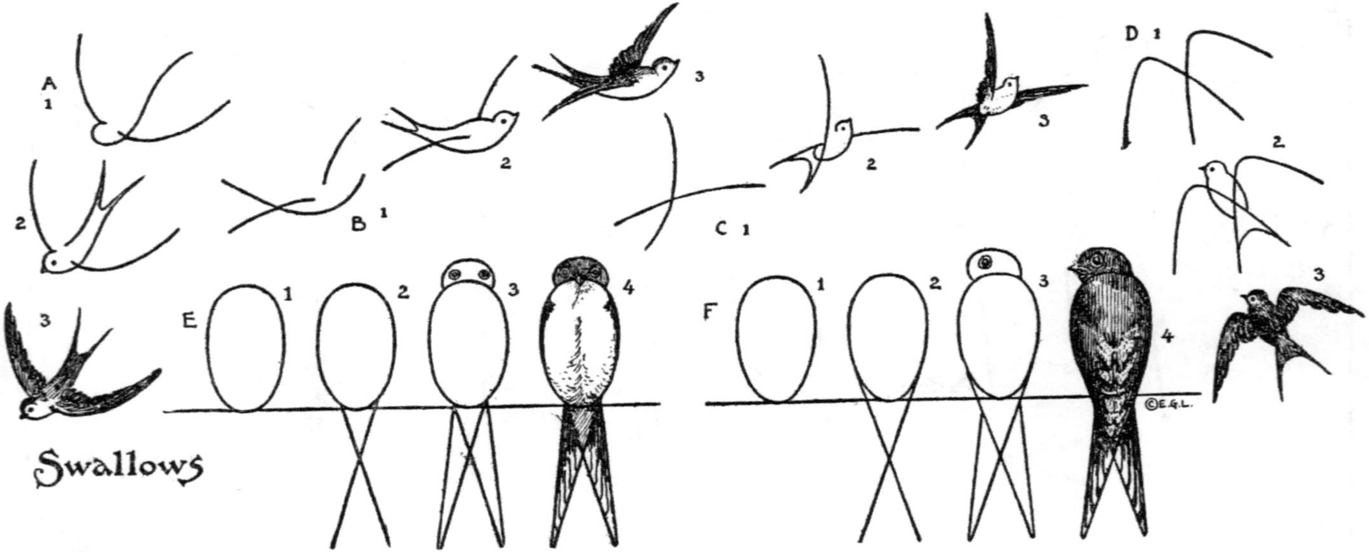

Swallows

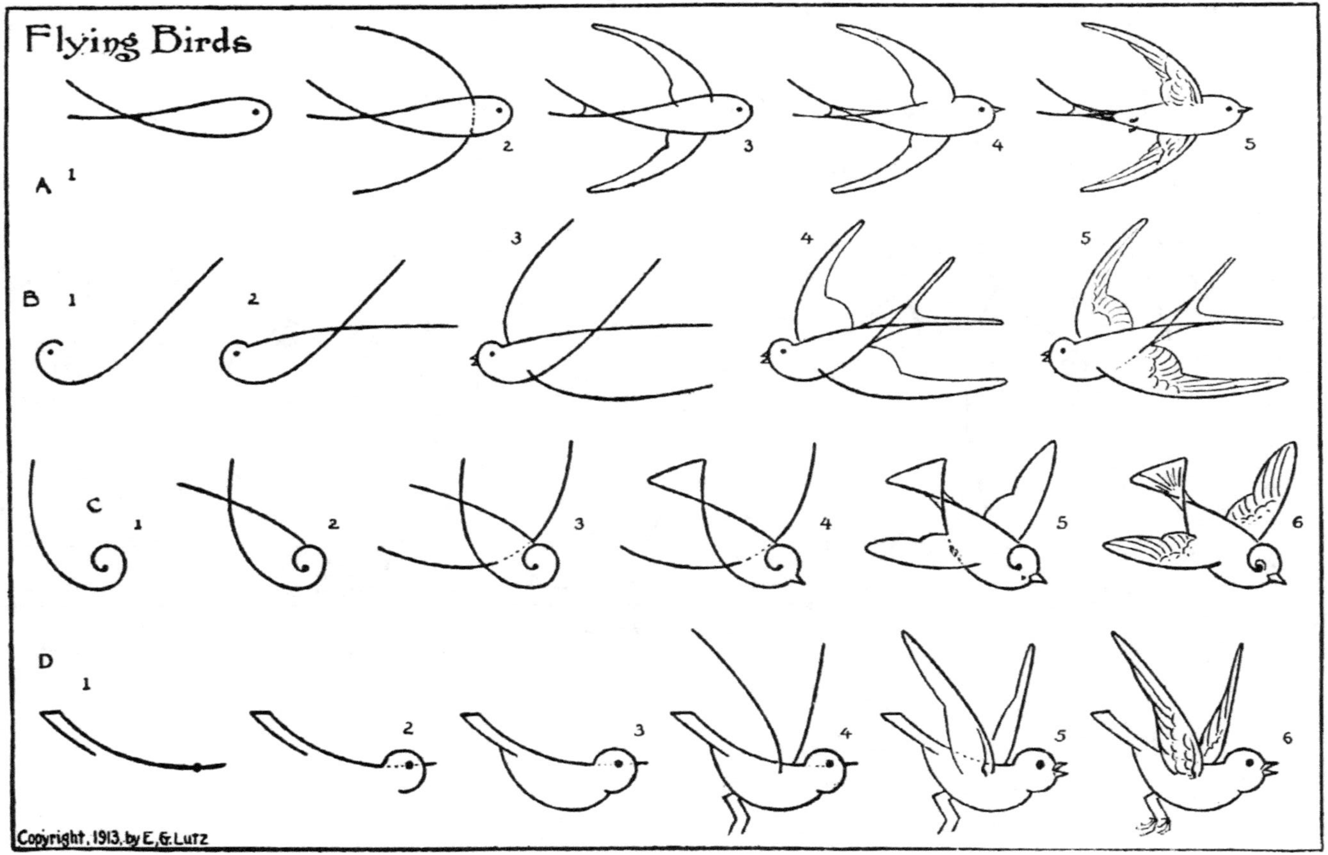

Flying Birds
A 1
2
3
4
5
B 1
2
3
4
5
C 1
2
3
4
5
6
D 1
2
3
4
5
6
Copyright, 1913, by E. G. Lutz

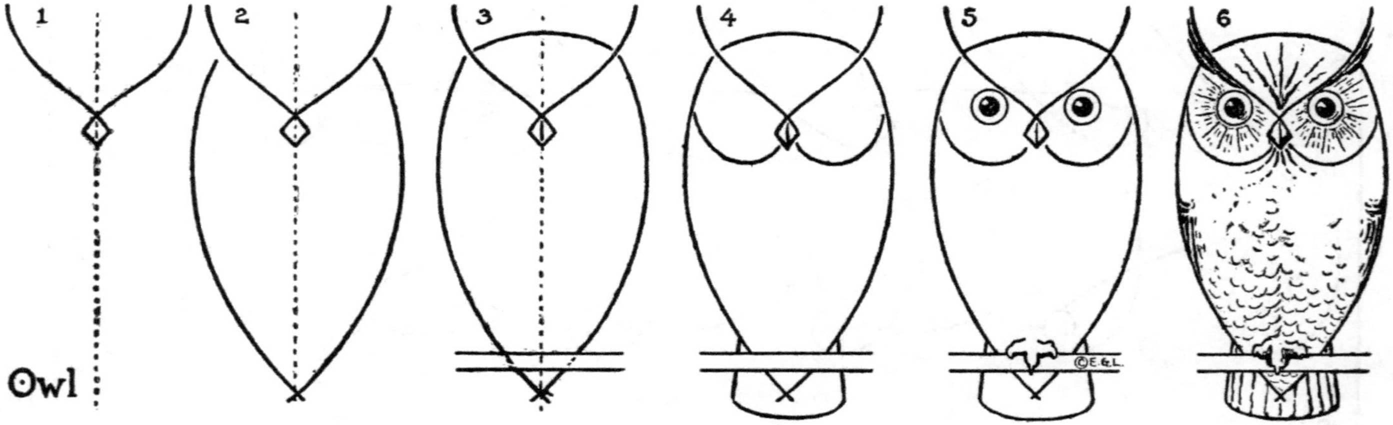
1
2
3
4
5
6
Owl
©E.&L.

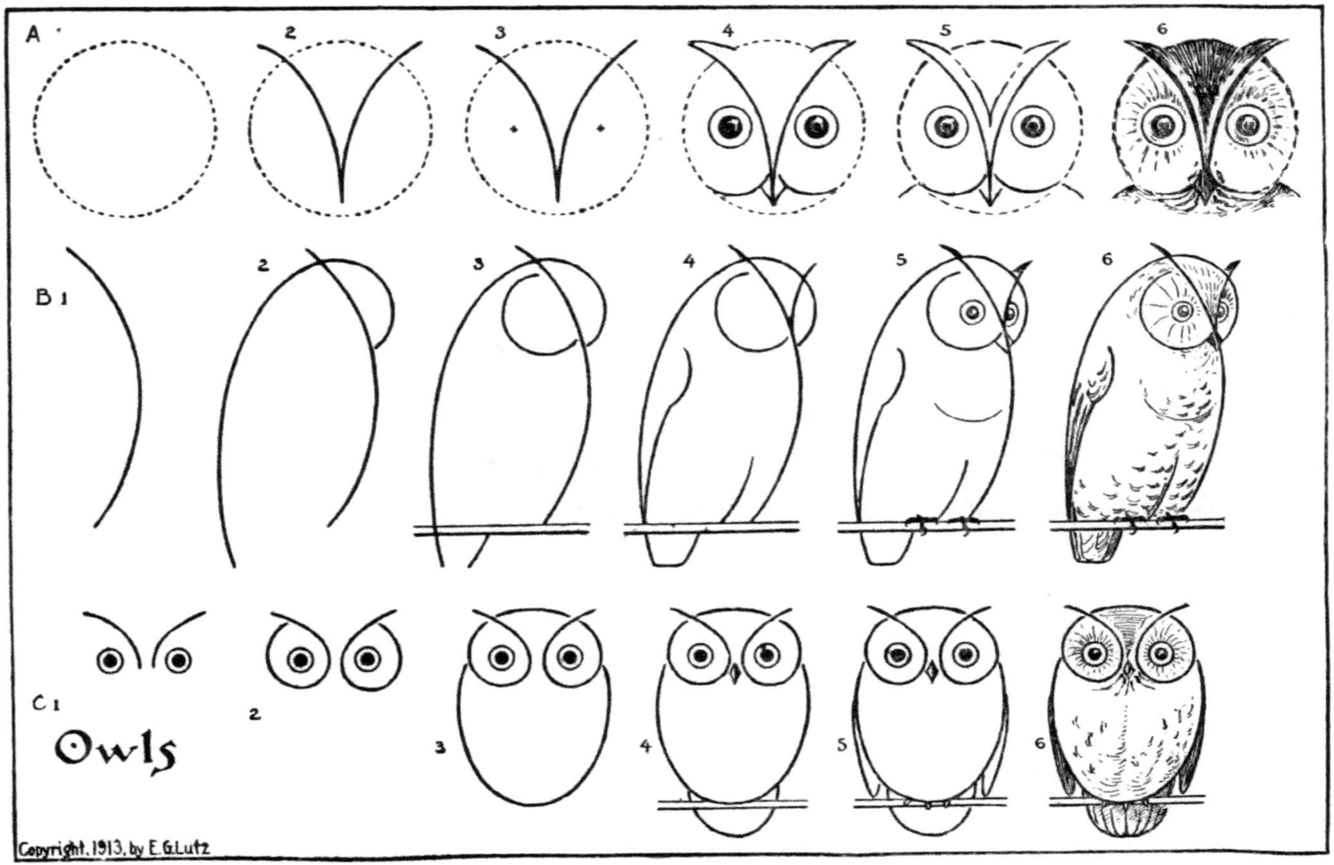

A
2
3
4
5
6
B 1
2
3
4
5
6
C 1
2
3
4
5
6
Owls
Copyright, 1913, by E.G.Lutz

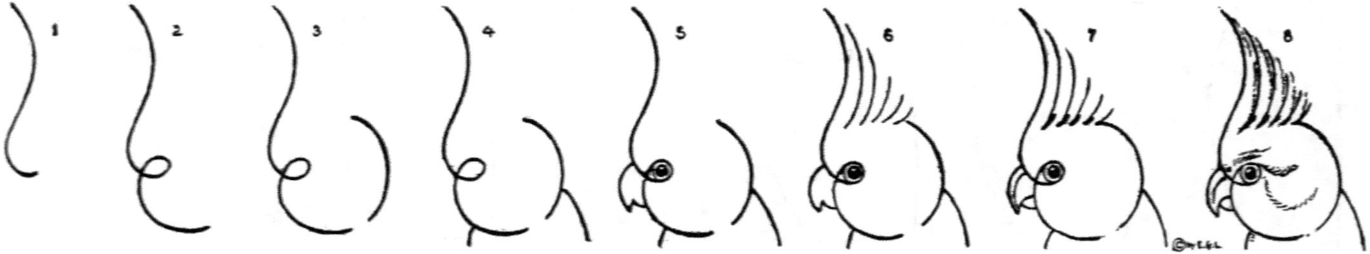
1
2
3
4
5
6
7
8

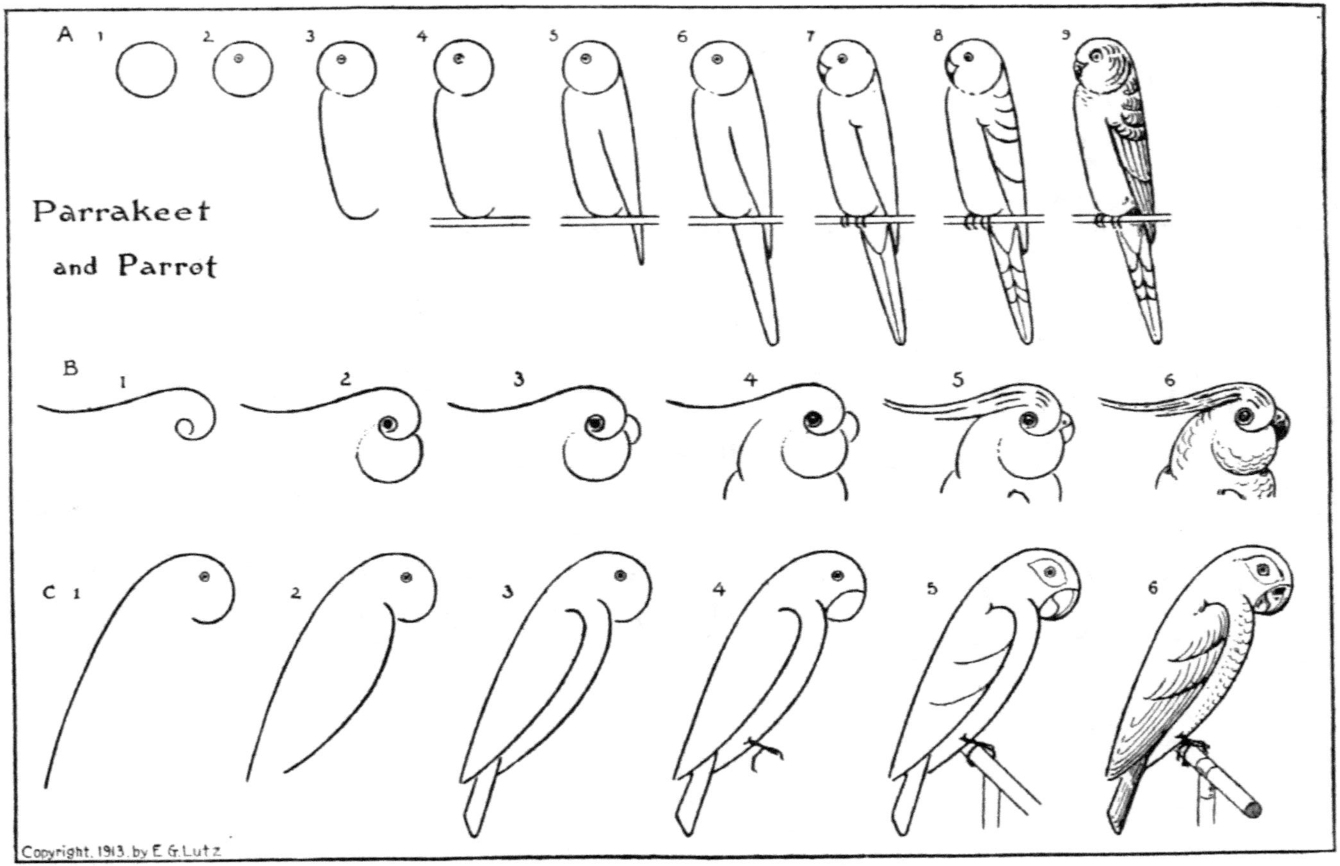
A 1
2
3
4
5
6
7
8
9
Parrakeet
and Parrot
B 1
2
3
4
5
6
C 1
2
3
4
5
6
Copyright. 1913. by E. G. Lutz

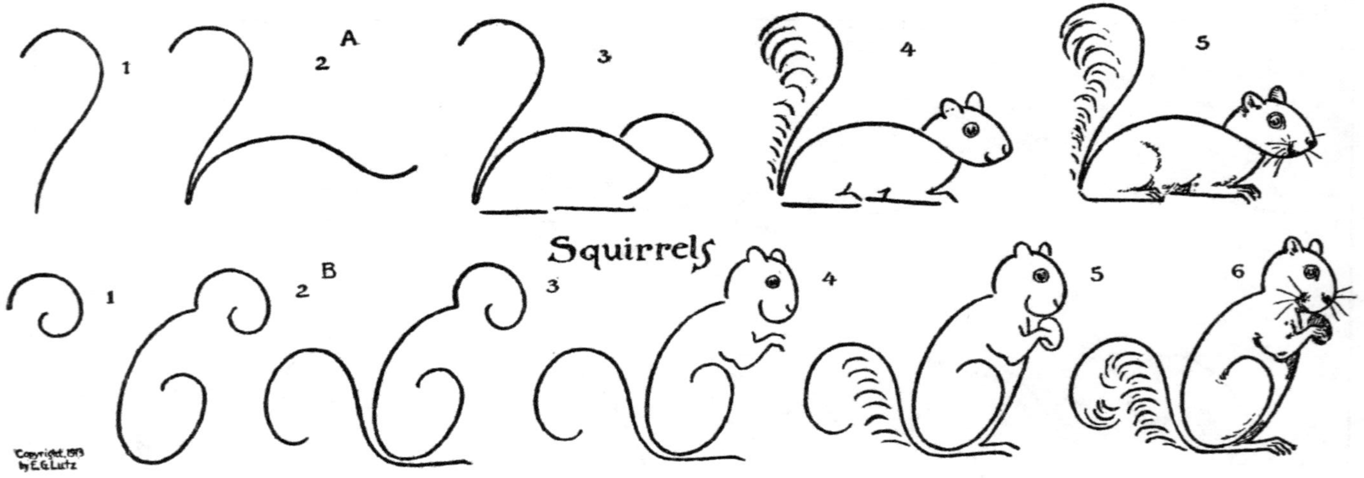
1
2
A
3
4
5
Squirrels
1
2
B
3
4
5
6
Copyright 1913 by E.G. Lutz

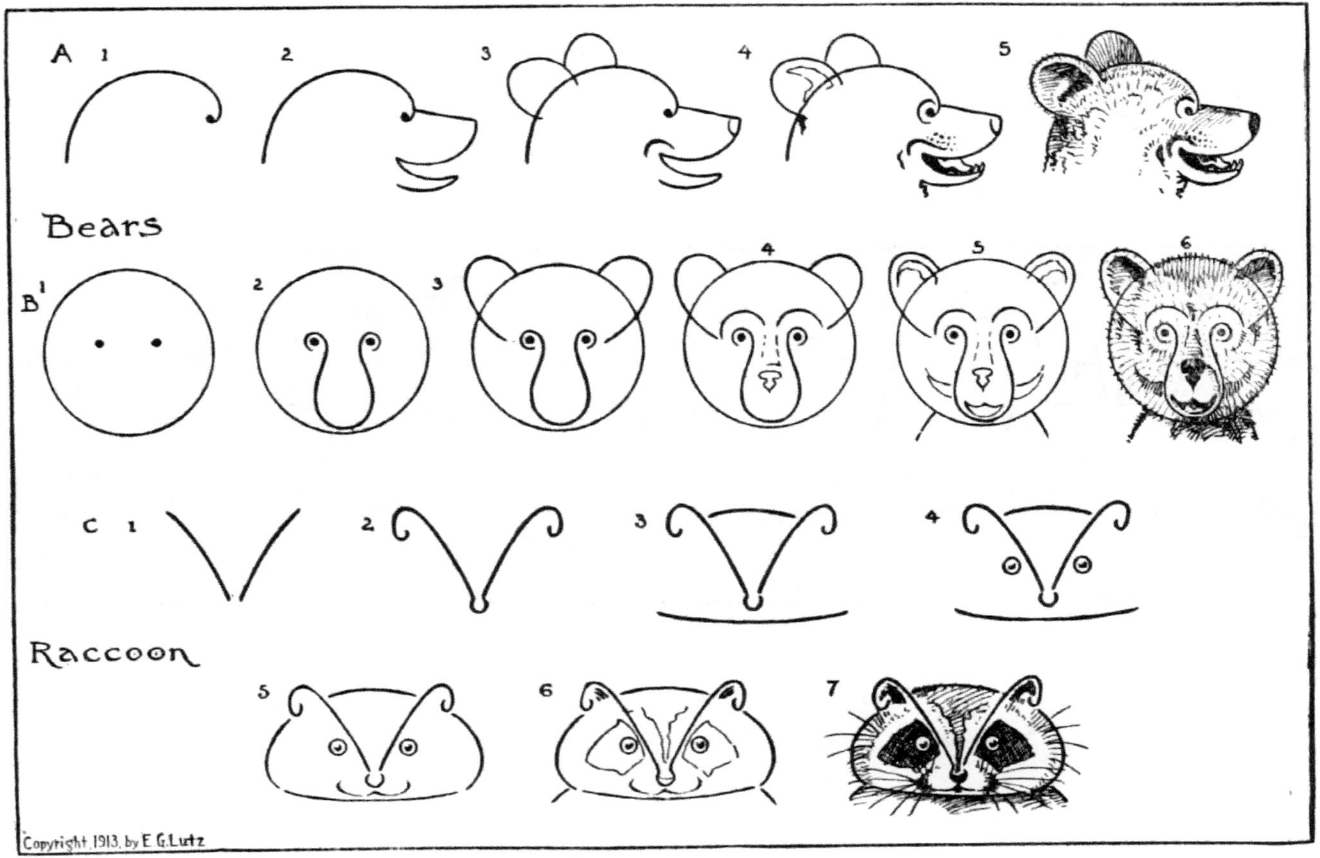
A 1
2
3
4
5
Bears
B 1
2
3
4
5
6
C 1
2
3
4
Raccoon
5
6
7
Copyright, 1913, by E. G. Lutz

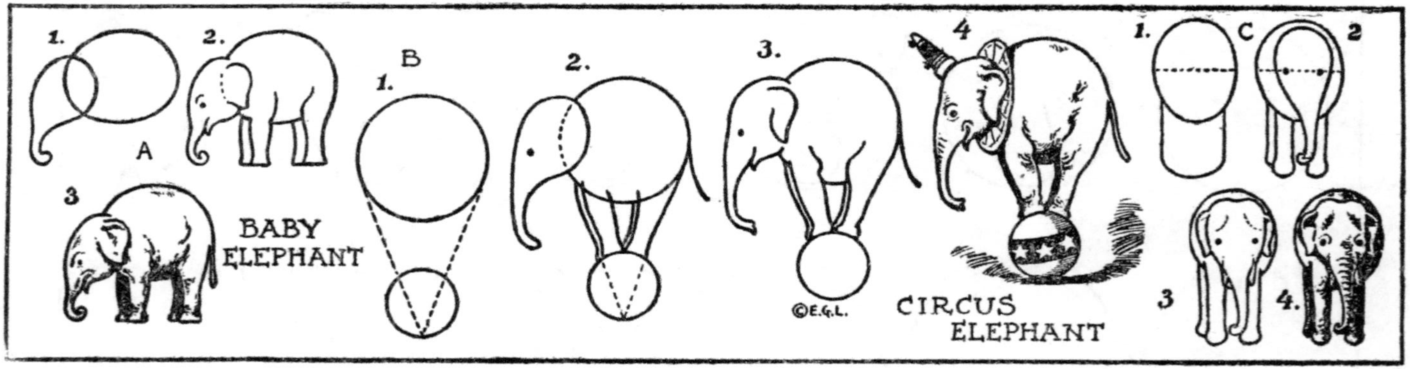
1.
2.
A
3
BABY
ELEPHANT
B
1.
2.
3.
©E.G.L.
4
CIRCUS
ELEPHANT
1.
C
2
3
4.

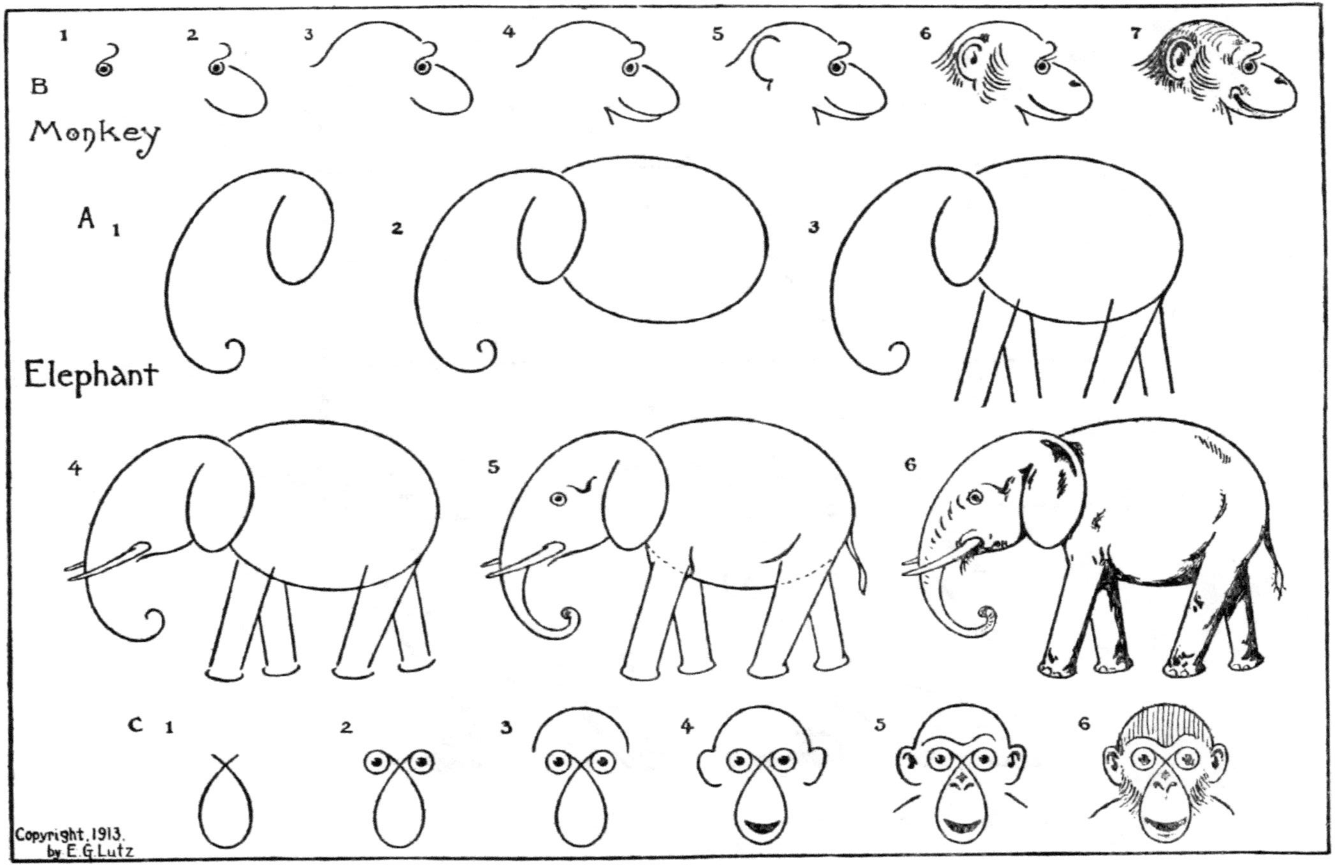
B
1
2
3
4
5
6
7
Monkey
A 1
2
3
Elephant
4
5
6
C 1
2
3
4
5
6
Copyright, 1913.
by E.G.Lutz

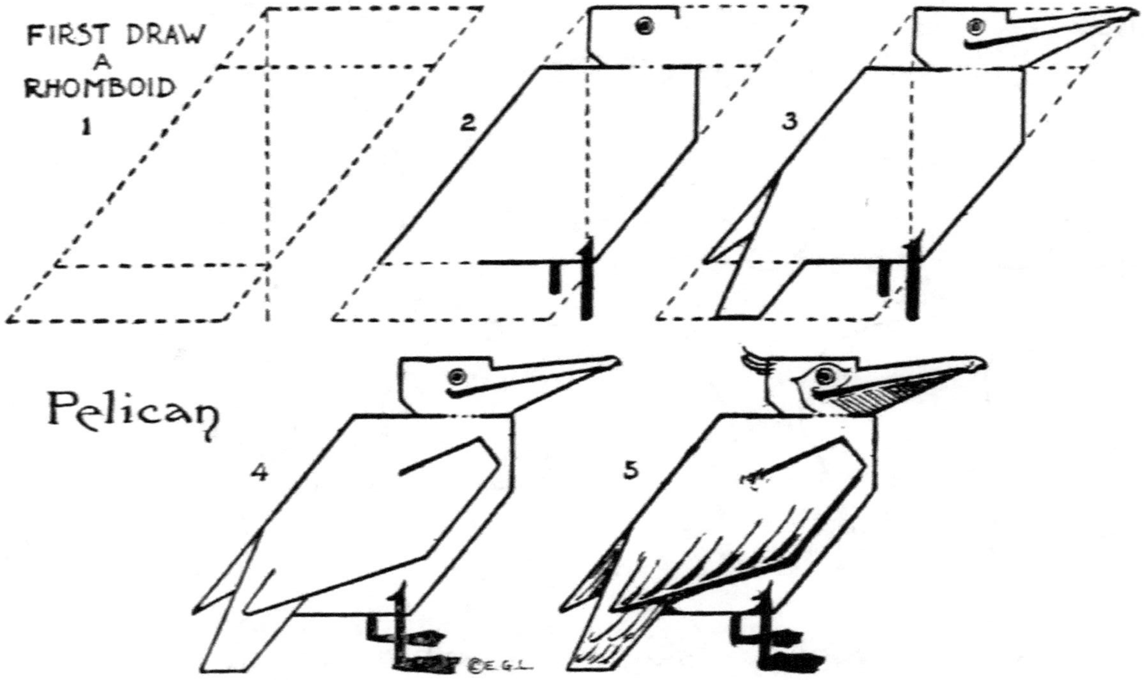
FIRST DRAW
A
RHOMBOID
1
2
3
Pelican
4
5
©E.G.L.

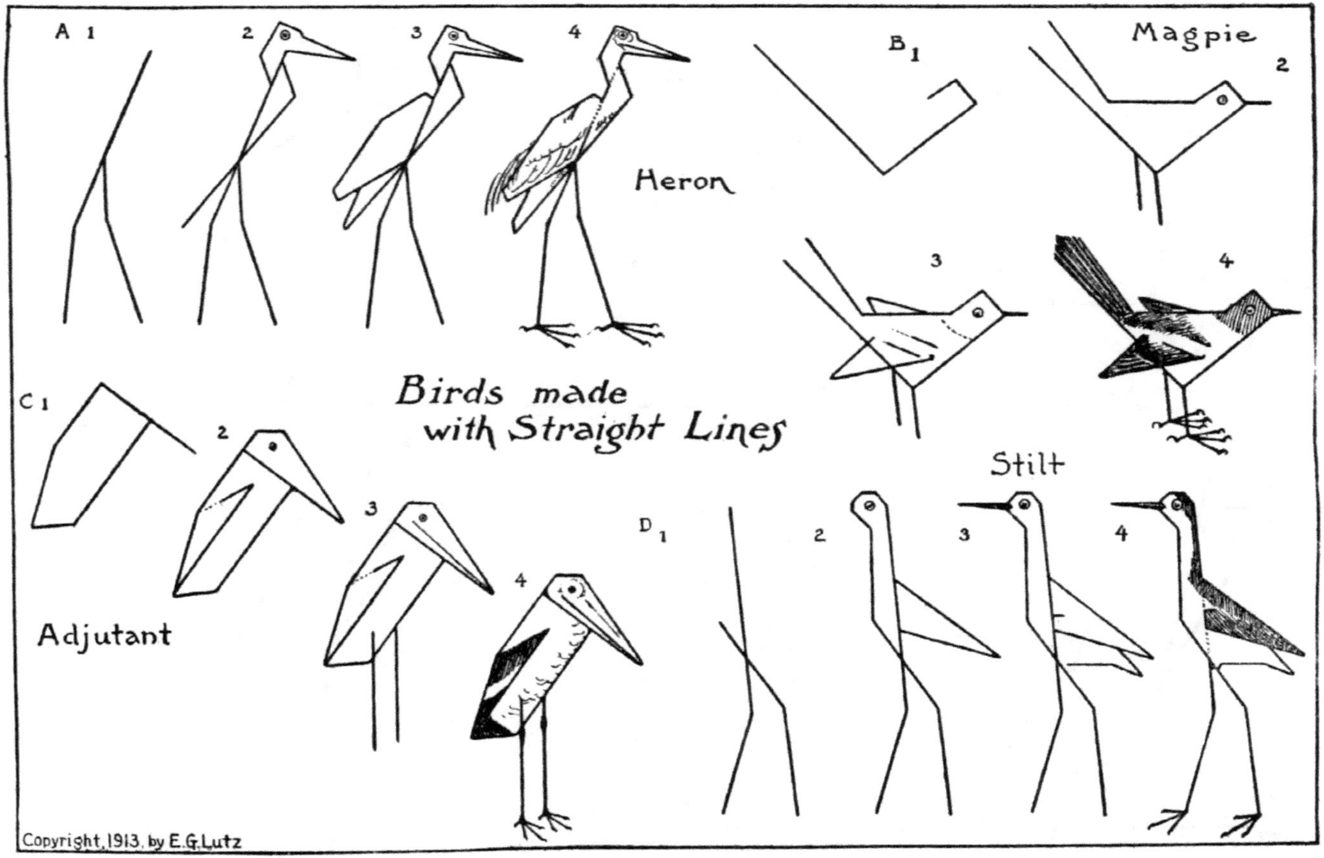
A 1
2
3
4
Heron
B 1
Magpie
2
3
4
Birds made with Straight Lines
C 1
2
3
4
Adjutant
D 1
2
3
4
Stilt
Copyright, 1913, by E.G.Lutz

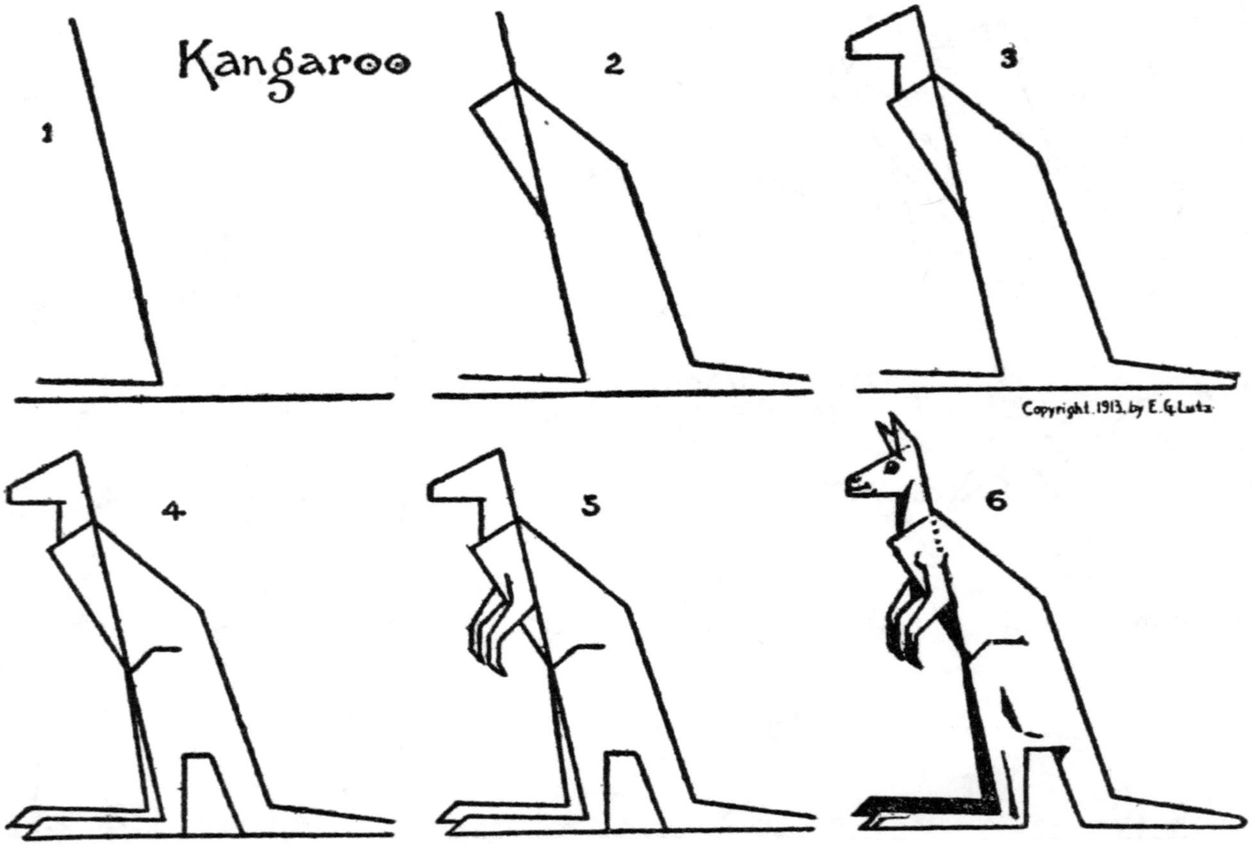
Kangaroo
1
2
3
4
5
6
Copyright. 1913, by E. G. Lutz

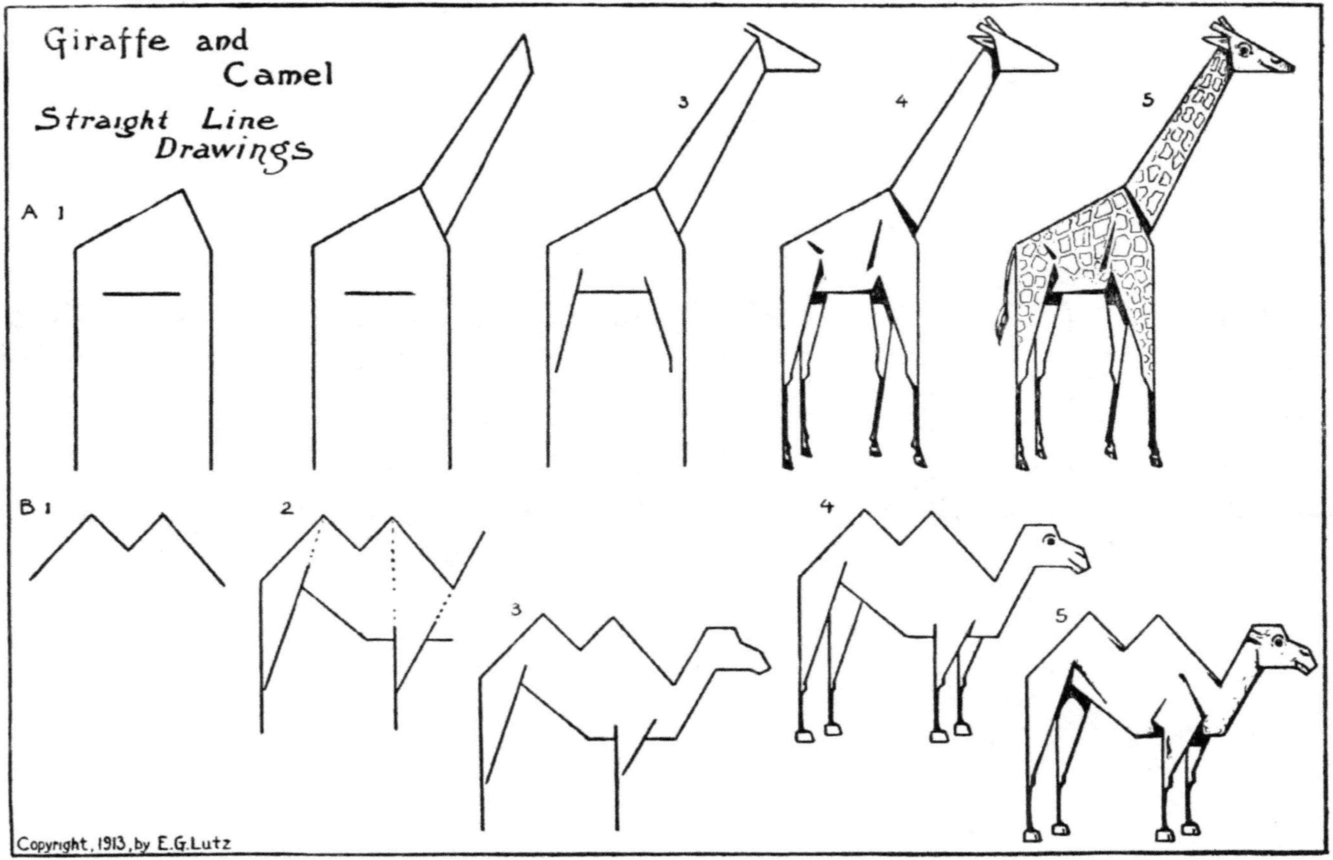
Giraffe and Camel
Straight Line Drawings
A 1
3
4
5
B 1
2
3
4
5
Copyright, 1913, by E.G.Lutz

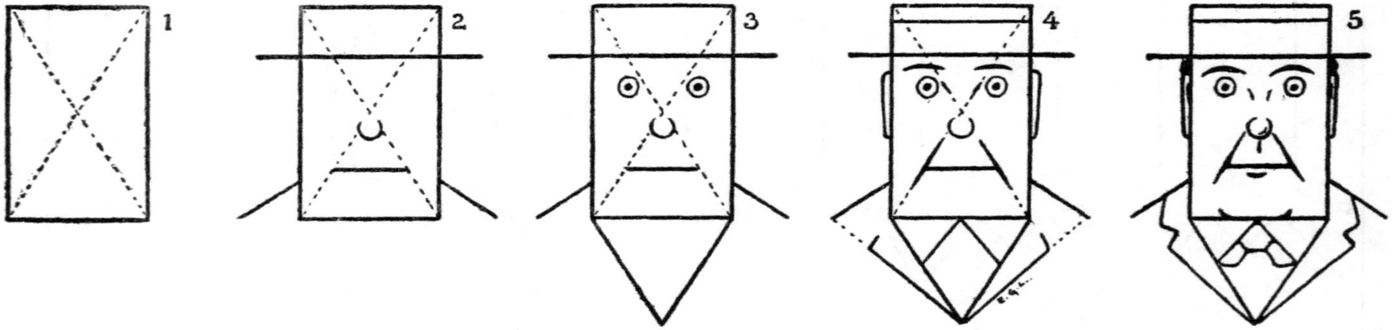
1
2
3
4
5

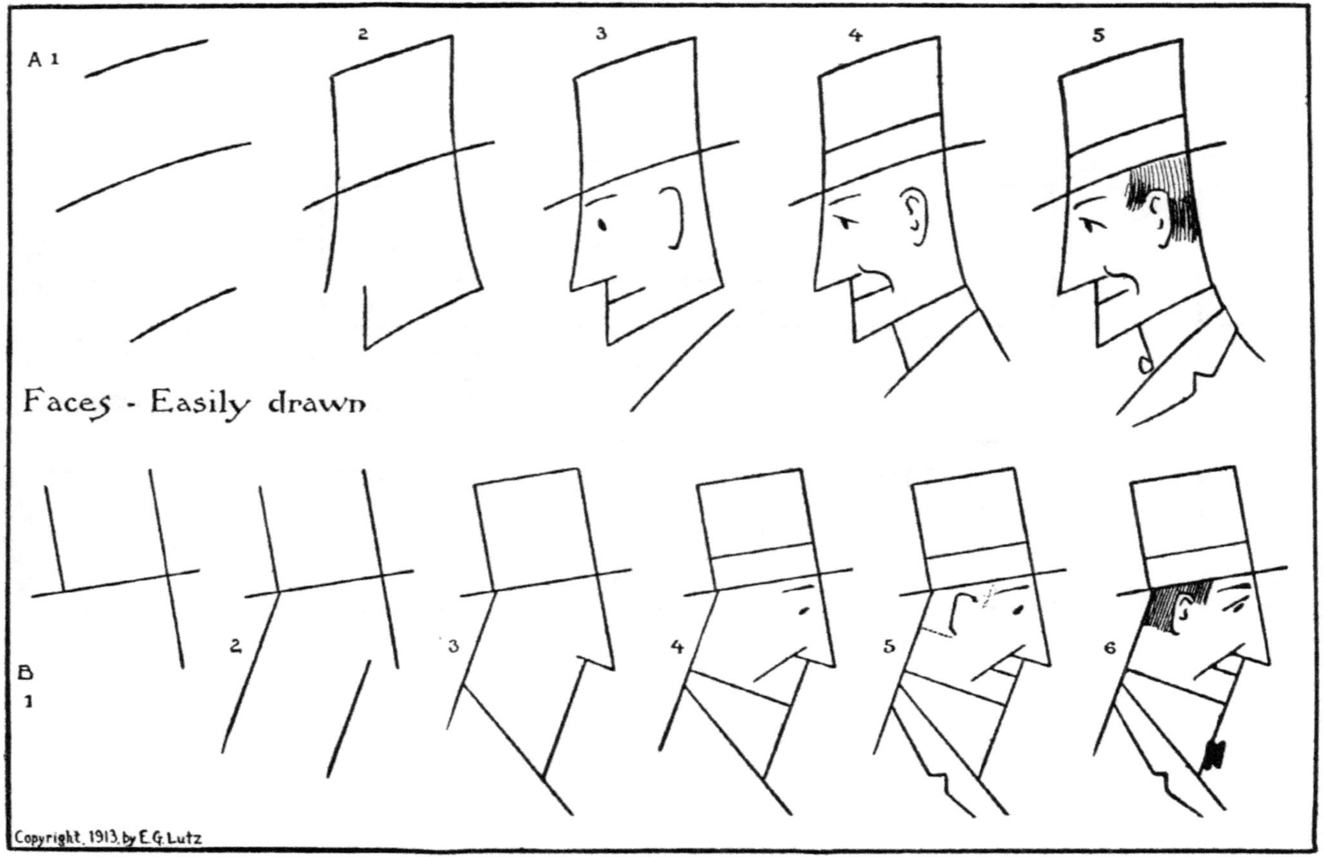
A 1
2
3
4
5
Faces - Easily drawn
B
1
2
3
4
5
6
Copyright, 1913, by E.G. Lutz

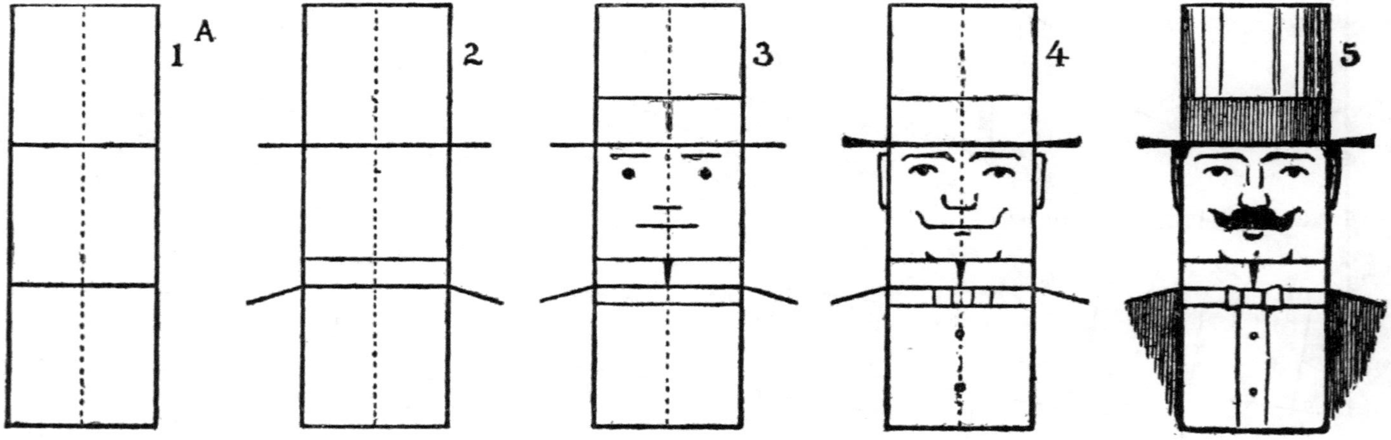
A
1
2
3
4
5

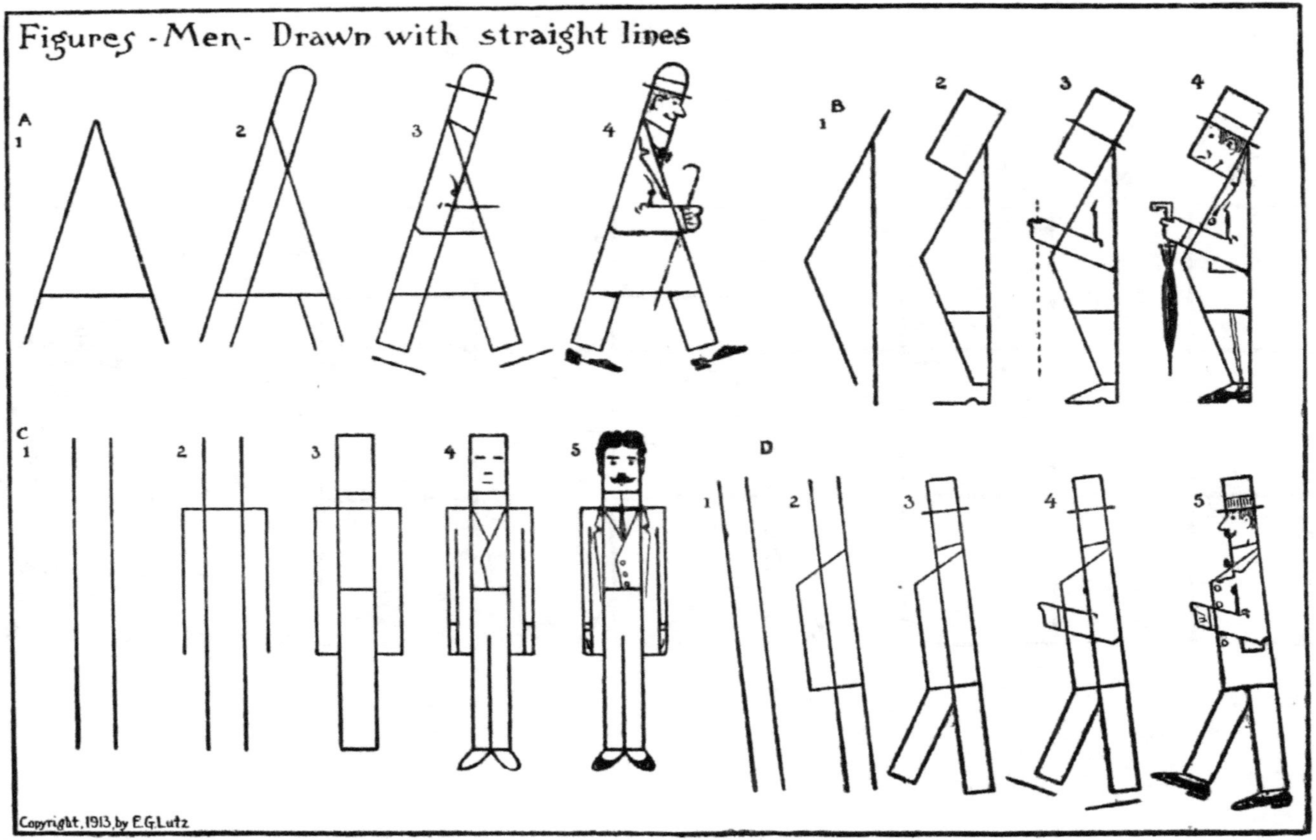
Figures - Men - Drawn with straight lines
A
1
2
3
4
B
1
2
3
4
C
1
2
3
4
5
D
1
2
3
4
5
Copyright, 1913, by E.G. Lutz

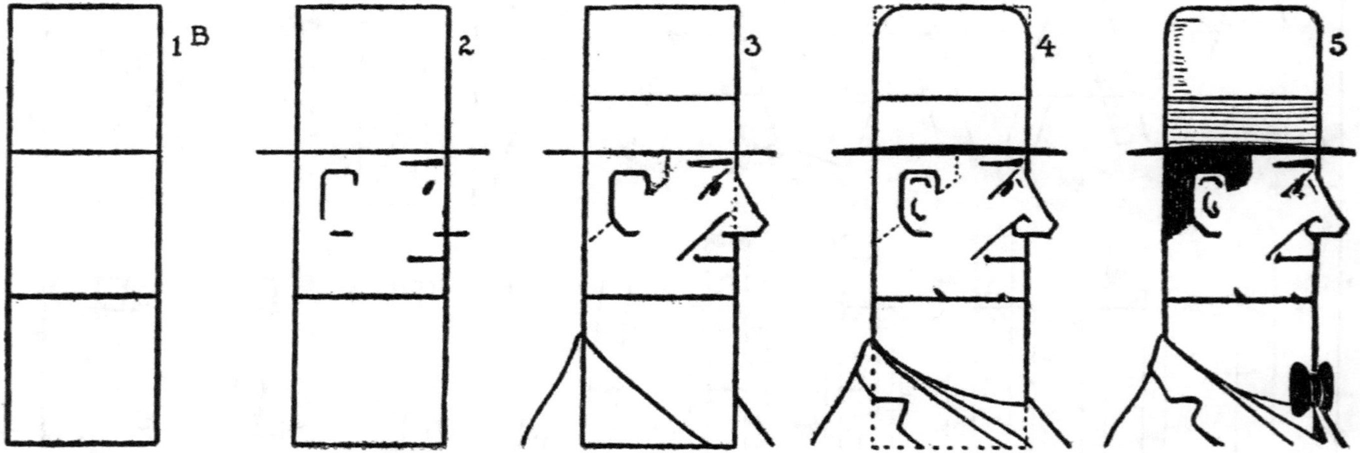
1 B
2
3
4
5

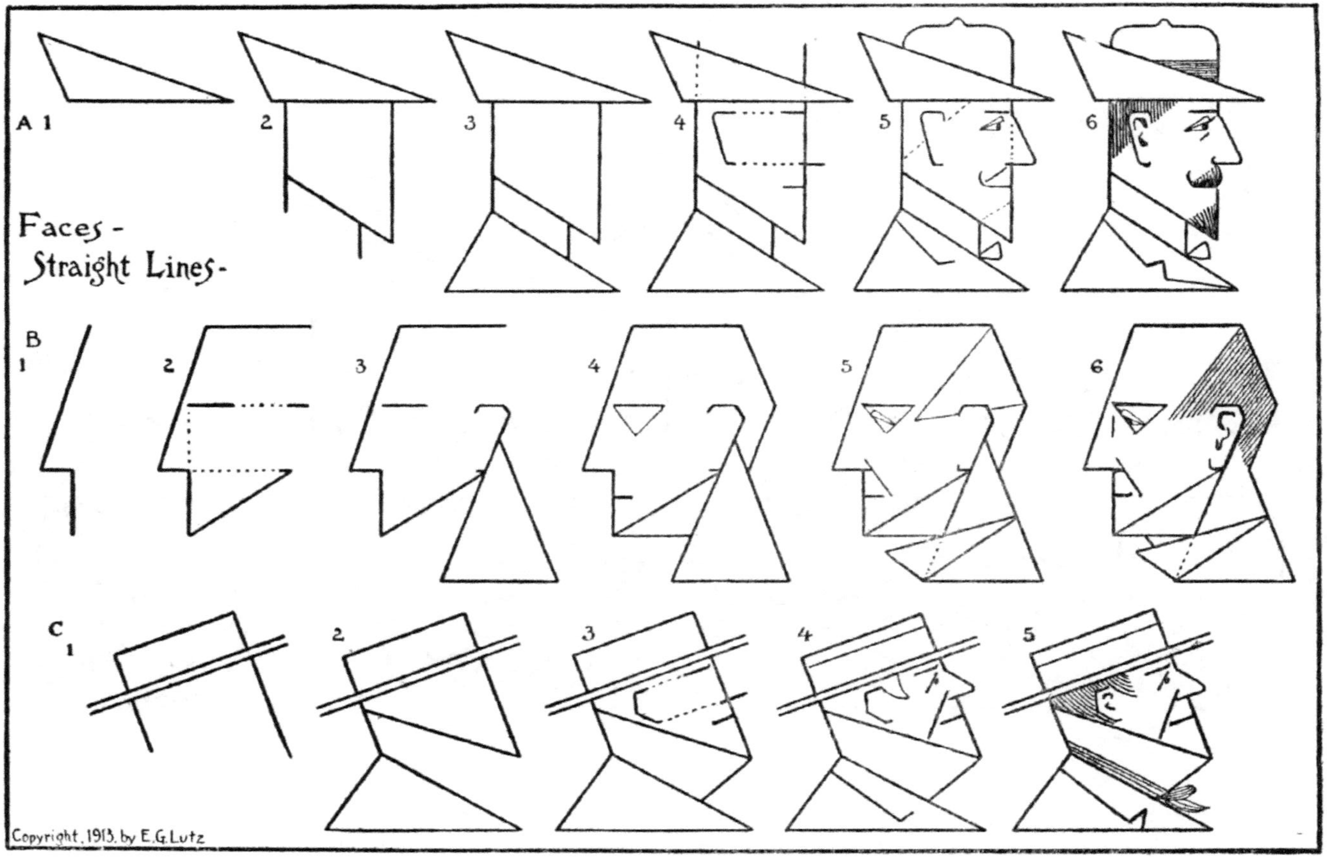

Faces -
Straight Lines -
A 1
2
3
4
5
6
B
1
2
3
4
5
6
C
1
2
3
4
5
Copyright, 1913, by E.G. Lutz

The Clown's Droll Face

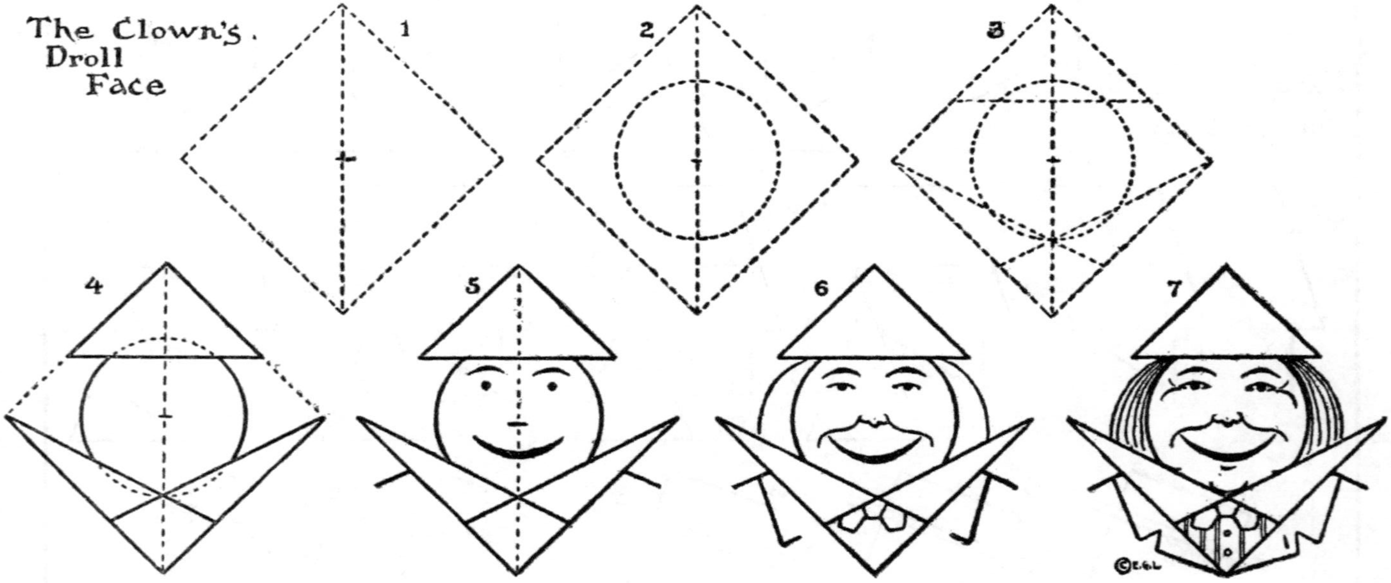

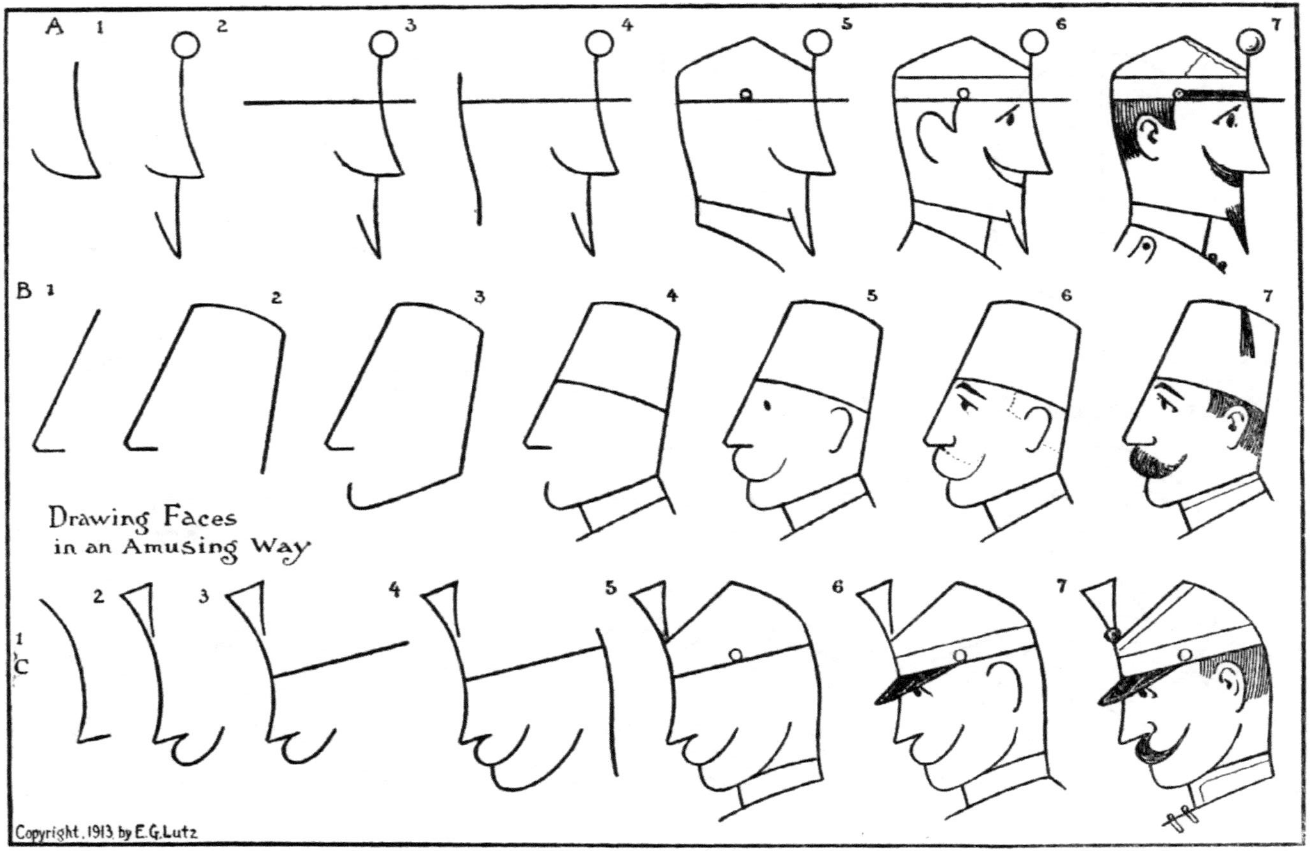
A 1 2 3 4 5 6 7
B 1 2 3 4 5 6 7
Drawing Faces
in an Amusing Way
C 1 2 3 4 5 6 7
Copyright, 1913, by E. G. Lutz

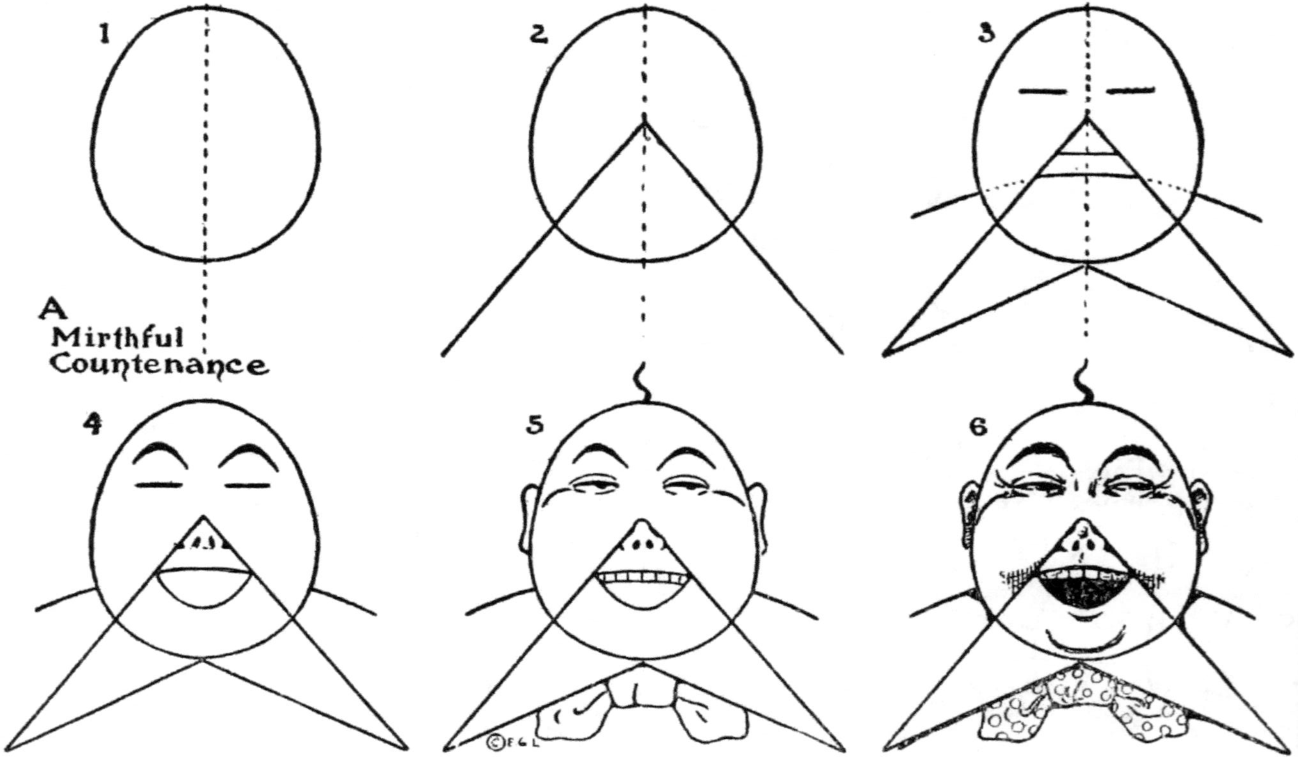
1
2
3
A Mirthful Countenance
4
5
6
©FGL

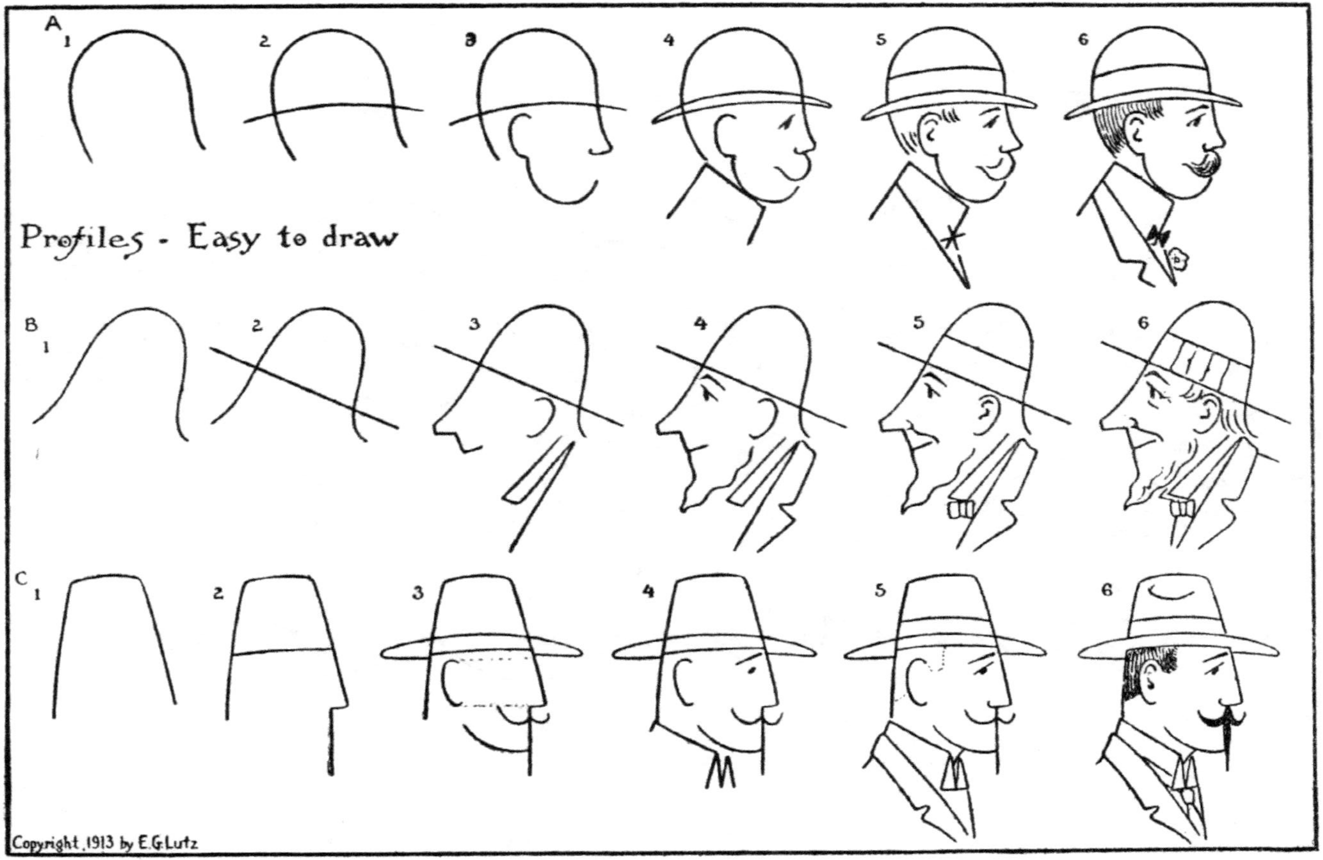
A 1
2
3
4
5
6
Profiles - Easy to draw
B 1
2
3
4
5
6
C 1
2
3
4
5
6
Copyright, 1913 by E.G.Lutz

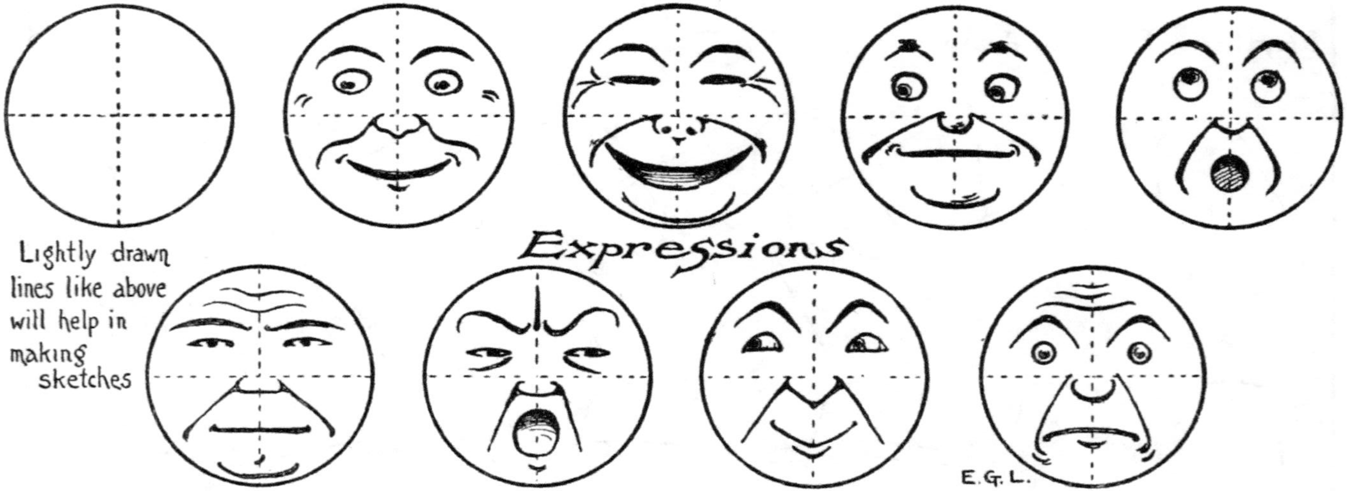
Expressions
Lightly drawn lines like above will help in making sketches
E. G. L.

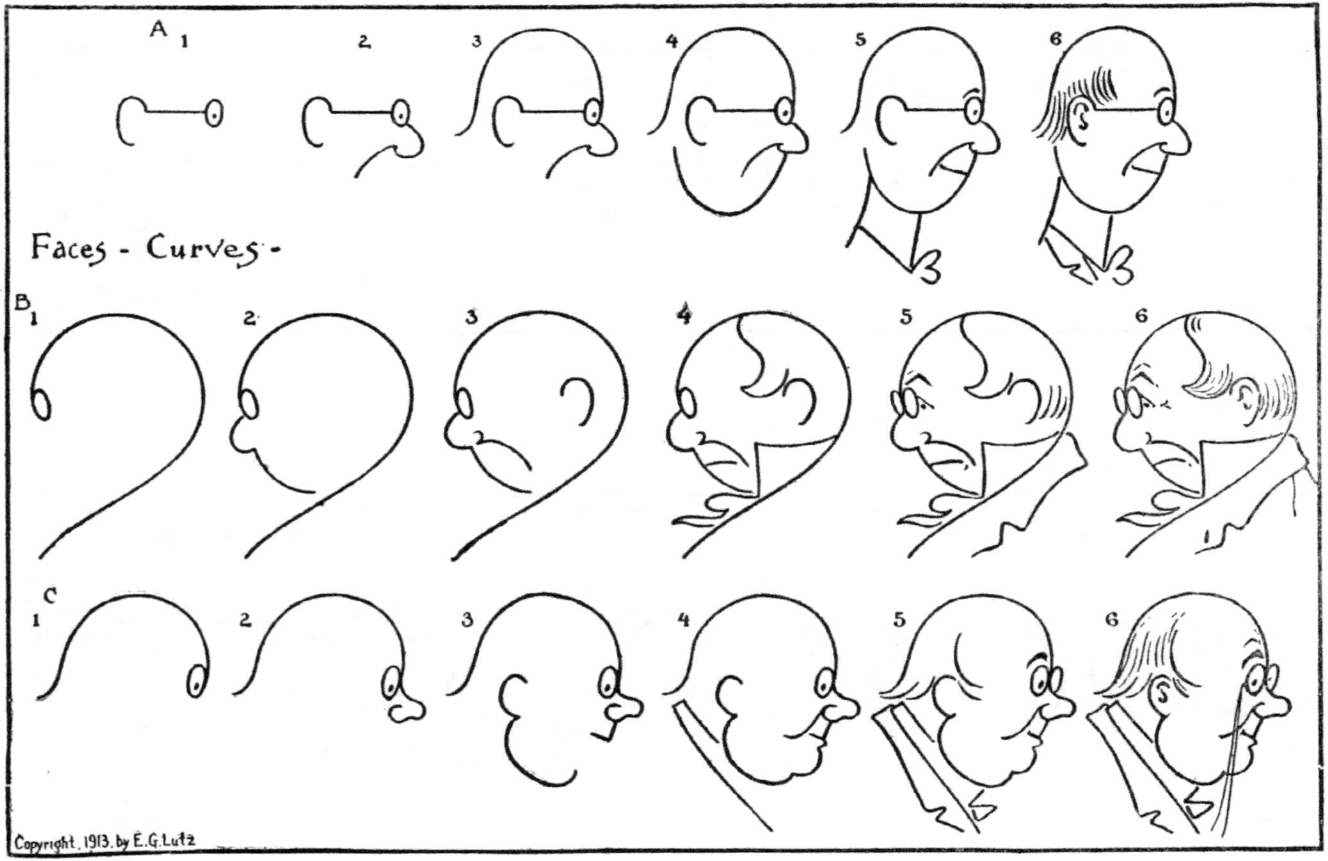
A
1
2
3
4
5
6
Faces - Curves -
B
1
2
3
4
5
6
C
1
2
3
4
5
6
Copyright, 1913, by E.G.Lutz

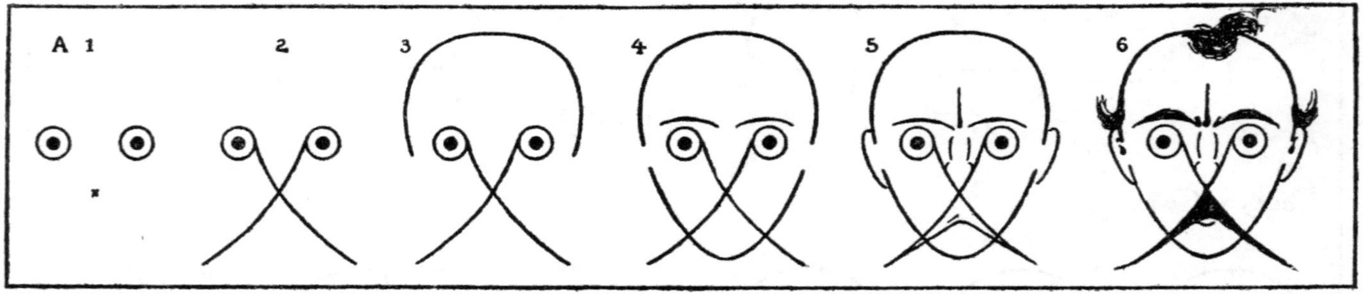
A 1
2
3
4
5
6

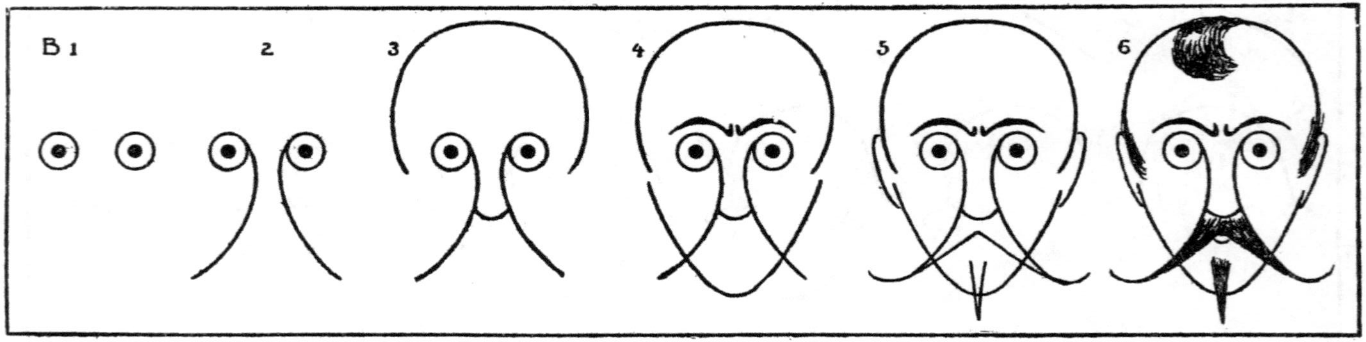
B 1
2
3
4
5
6

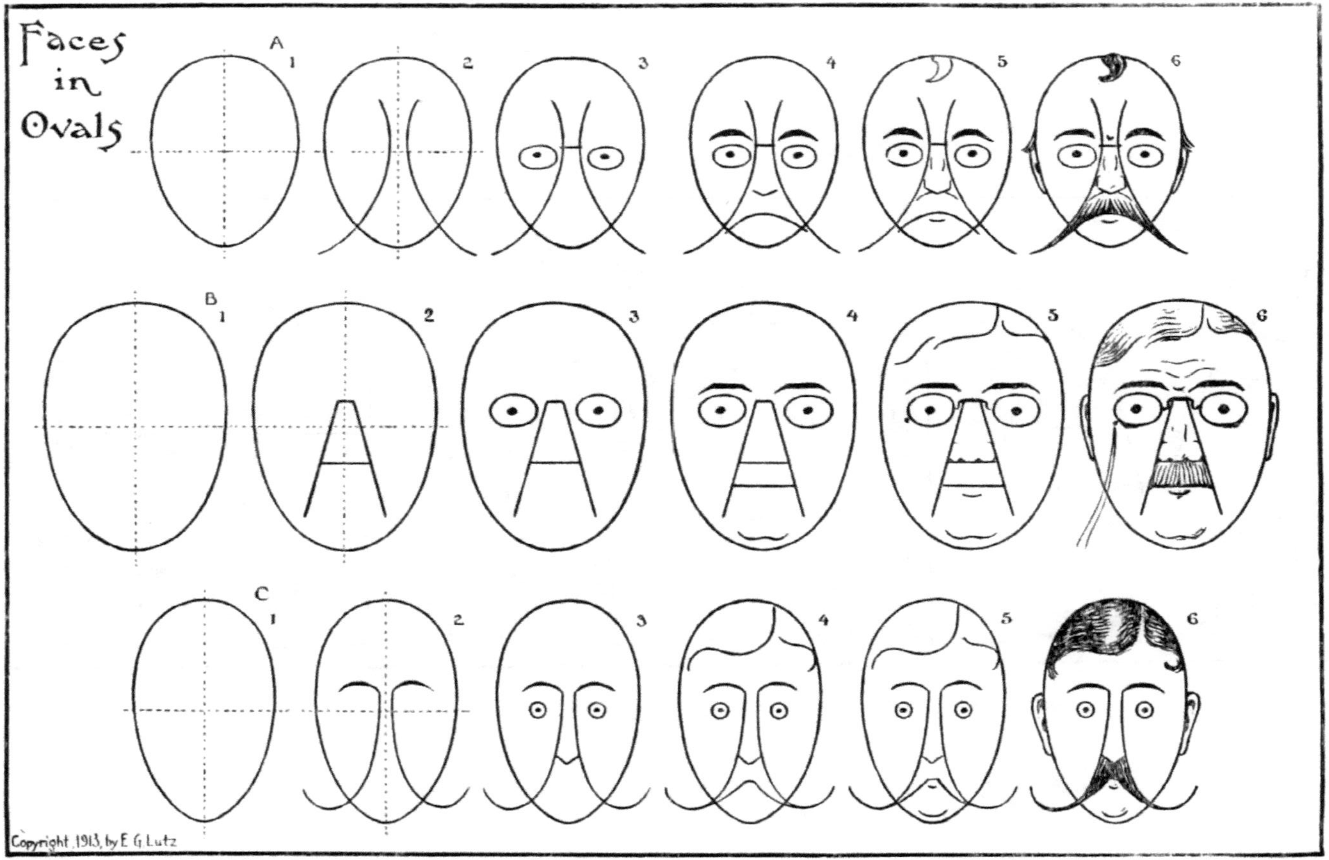
Faces in Ovals
A 1
2
3
4
5
6
B 1
2
3
4
5
6
C 1
2
3
4
5
6
Copyright, 1913, by E. G. Lutz

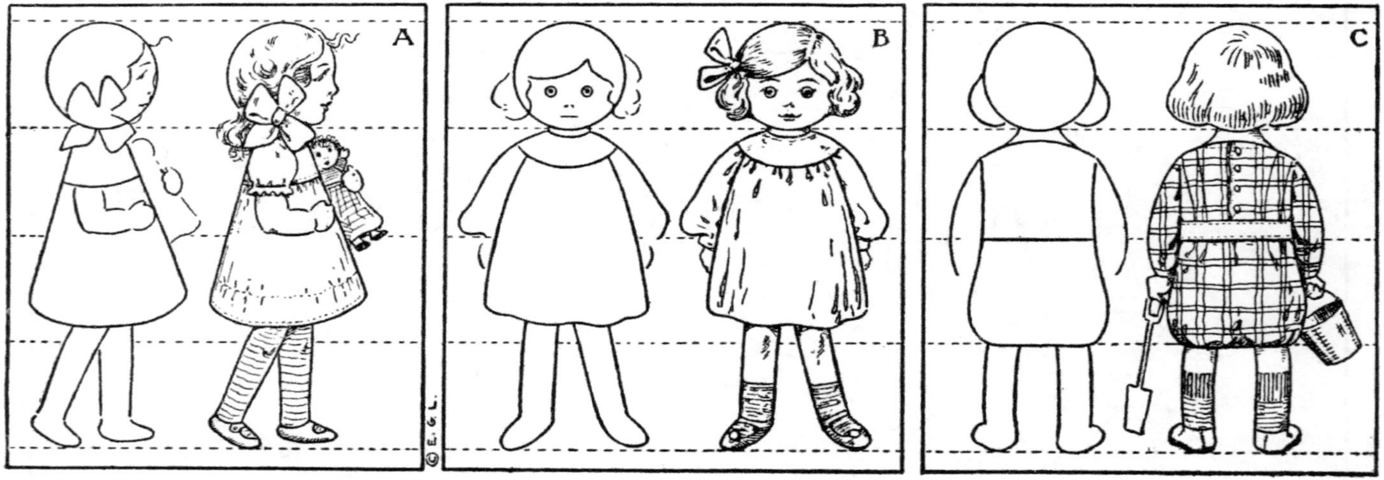
A
B
C
© E. G. L.

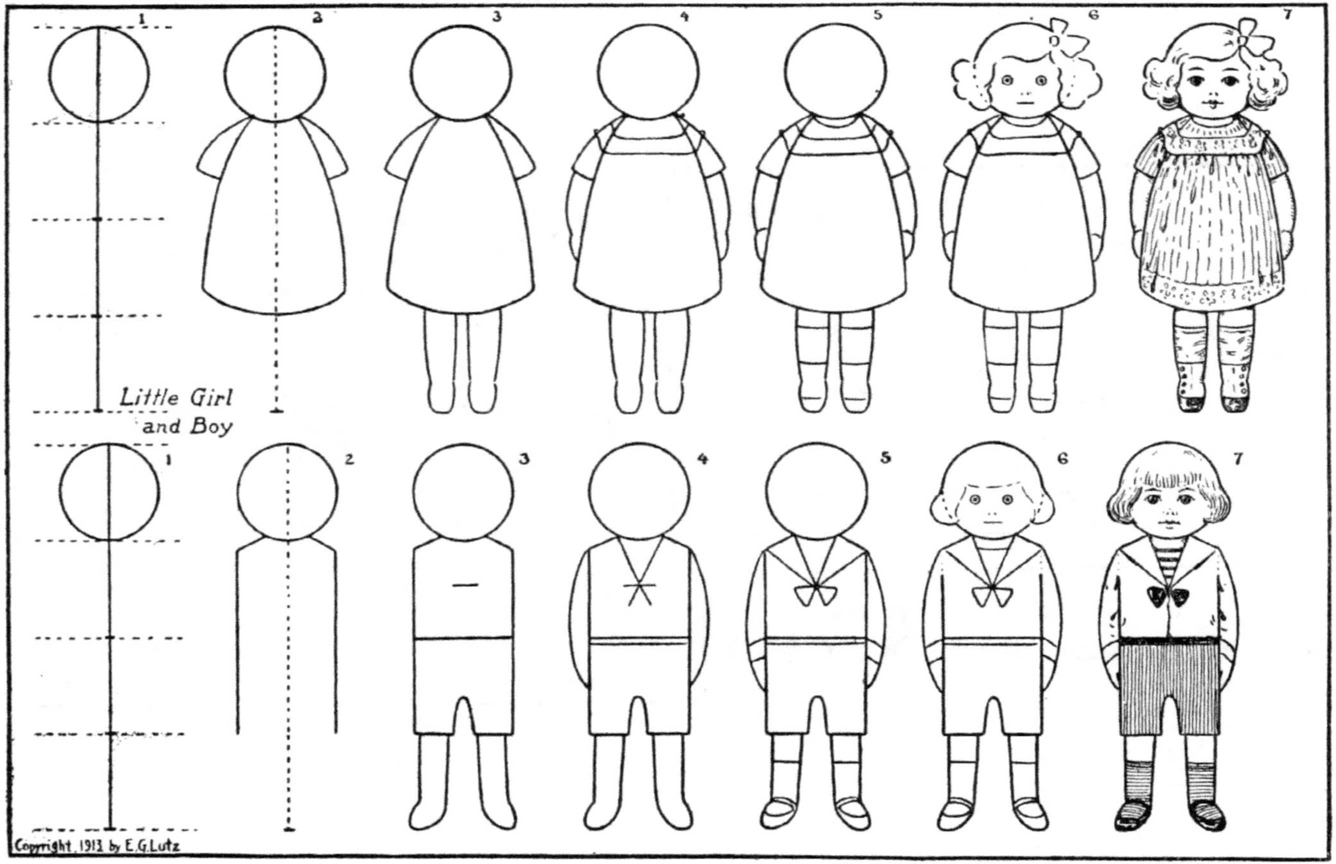
1
2
3
4
5
6
7
Little Girl
and Boy
1
2
3
4
5
6
7
Copyright, 1913, by E. G. Lutz

Round Figures

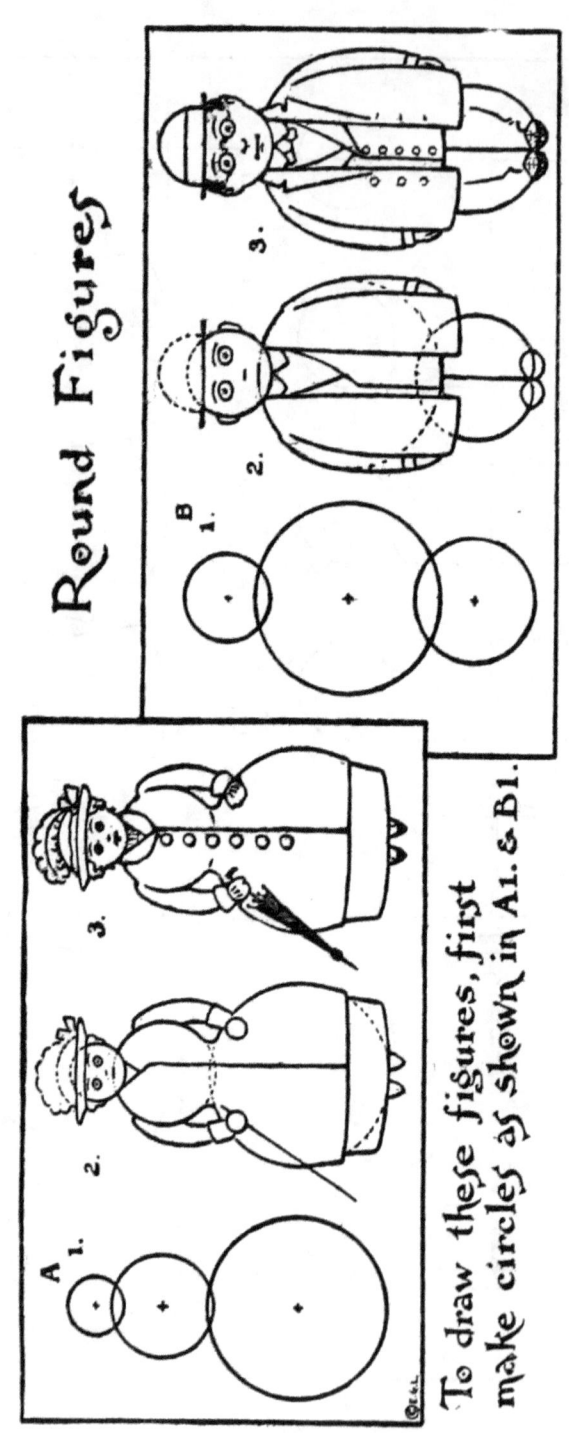

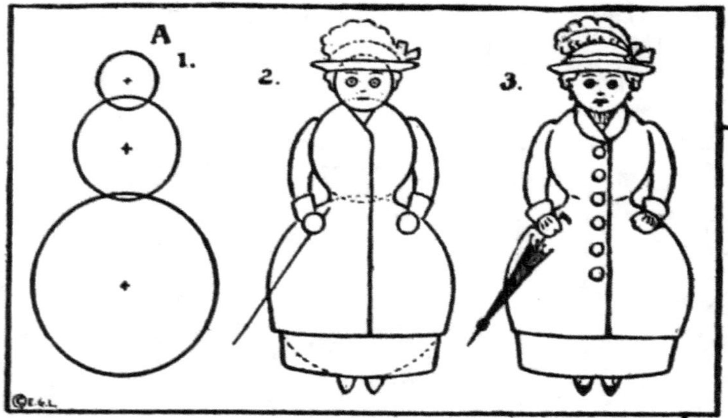

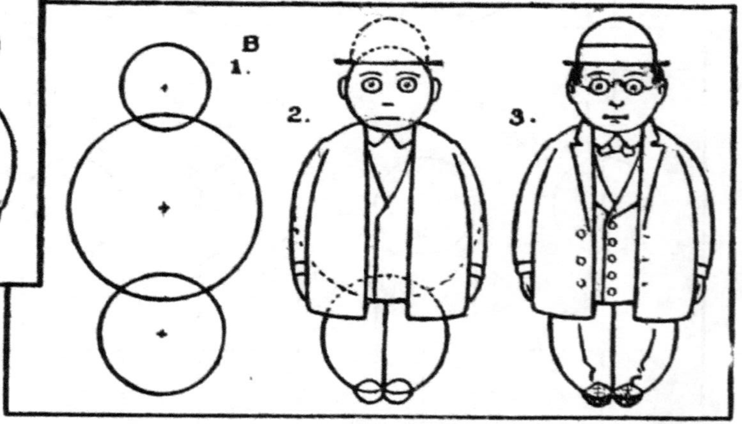

To draw these figures, first make circles as shown in A1. & B1.

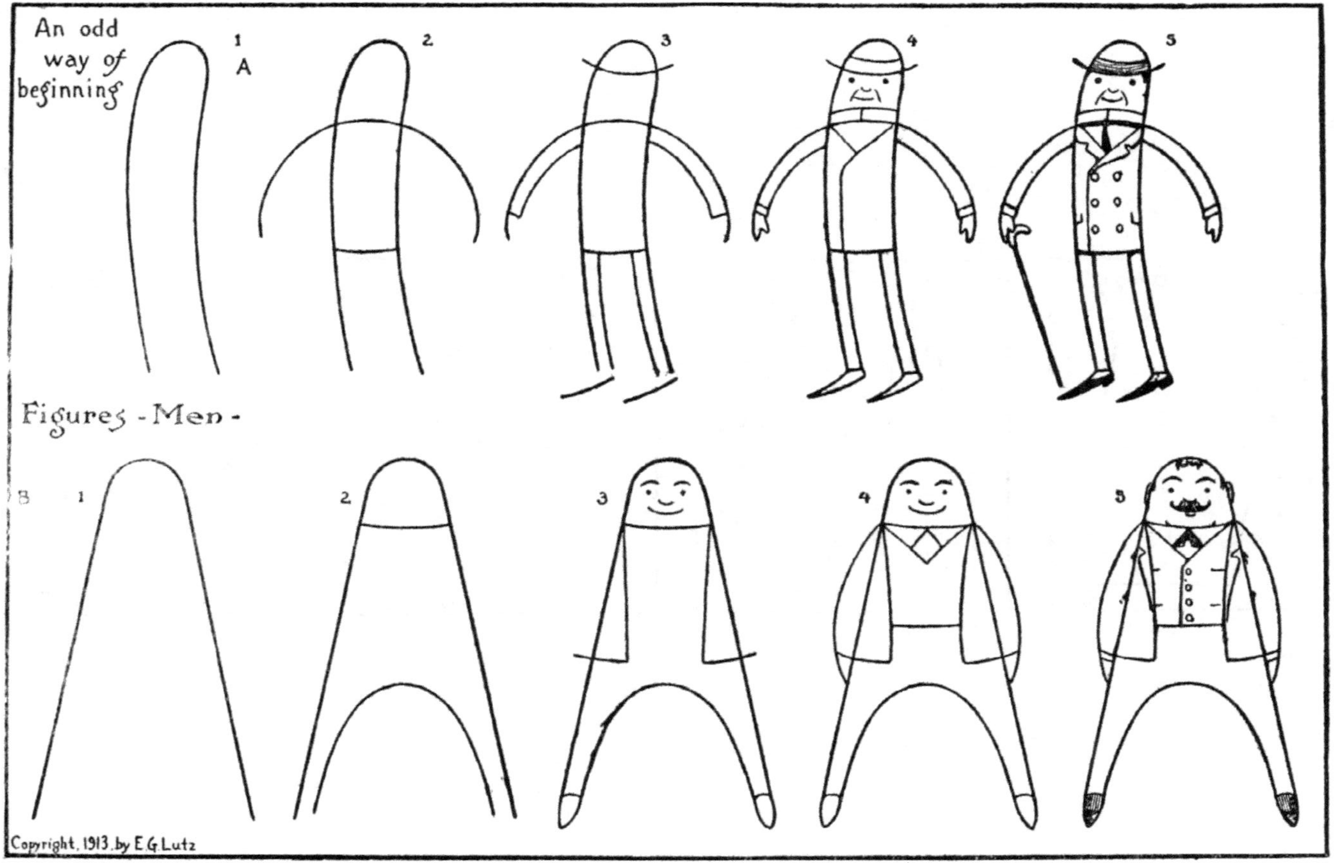
An odd way of beginning
1
A
2
3
4
5
Figures - Men -
B
1
2
3
4
5
Copyright, 1913, by E.G.Lutz

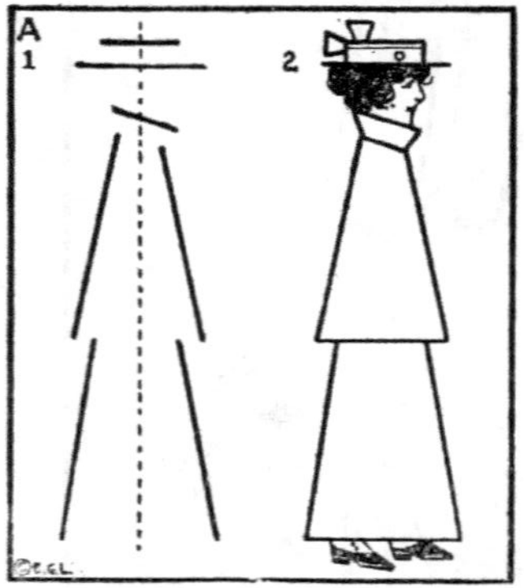
A
1
2

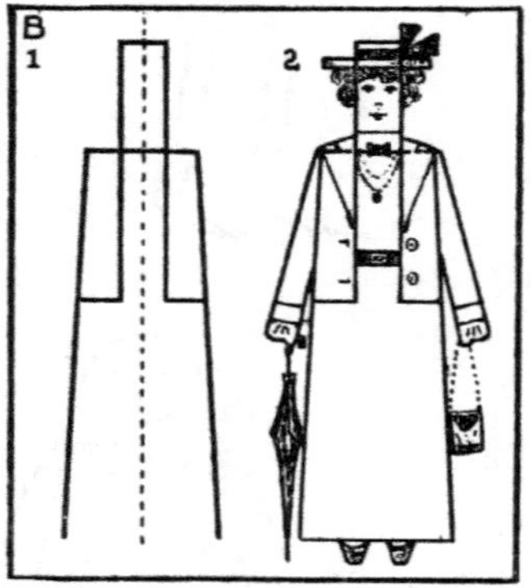
B
1
2

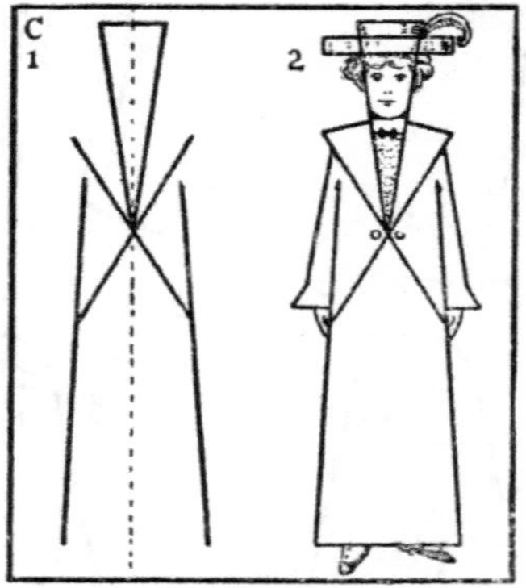
C
1
2

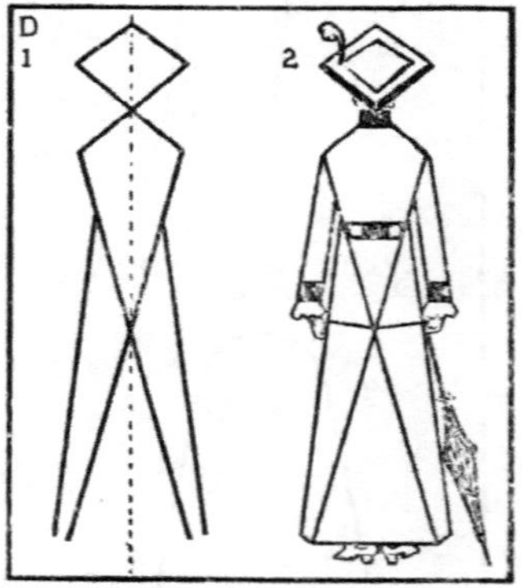
D
1
2

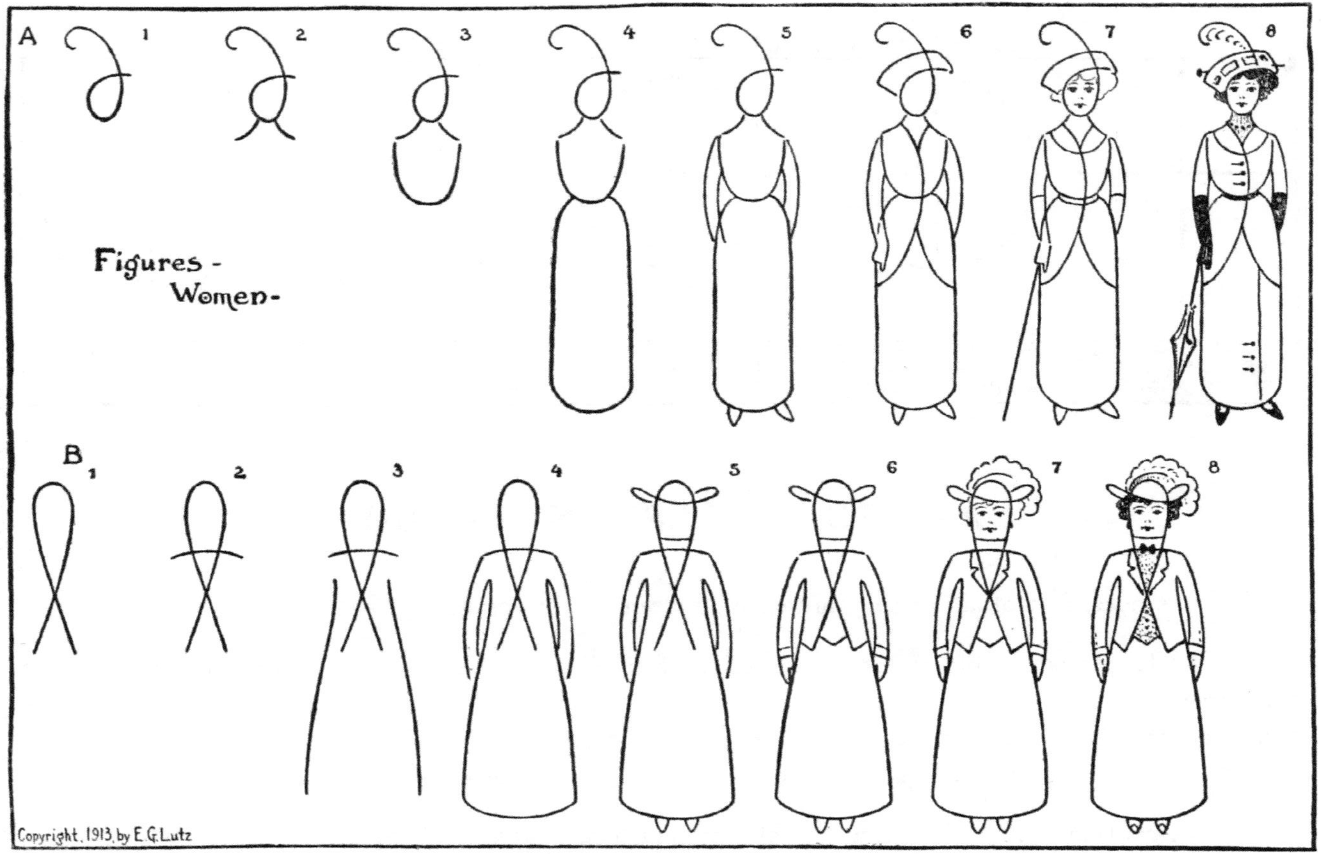
A
1
2
3
4
5
6
7
8
Figures - Women-
B
1
2
3
4
5
6
7
8
Copyright, 1913, by E. G. Lutz

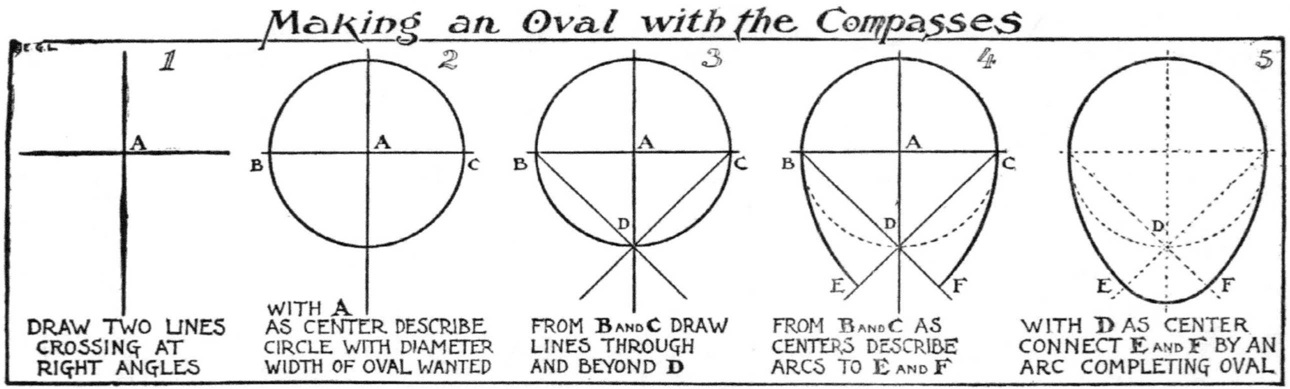
Making an Oval with the Compasses
1
2
3
4
5
A
B
C
D
E
F
DRAW TWO LINES CROSSING AT RIGHT ANGLES
WITH A AS CENTER DESCRIBE CIRCLE WITH DIAMETER WIDTH OF OVAL WANTED
FROM B AND C DRAW LINES THROUGH AND BEYOND D
FROM B AND C AS CENTERS DESCRIBE ARCS TO E AND F
WITH D AS CENTER CONNECT E AND F BY AN ARC COMPLETING OVAL

DRAWING OVALS AND ELLIPSES

Take note, first of all, of the difference between an ellipse and an oval.

The large plate explains the construction of an ellipse. It shows how to find the points where the three pins are placed that determine the size of the looped string. Be sure and make measurements accurately. Use a string that will not give, cotton thread is good for small ellipses, silk is too elastic. A suggestion to amateur gardeners: make elliptical flower beds this way.

The caution in regard to accuracy also applies to the making of the oval.

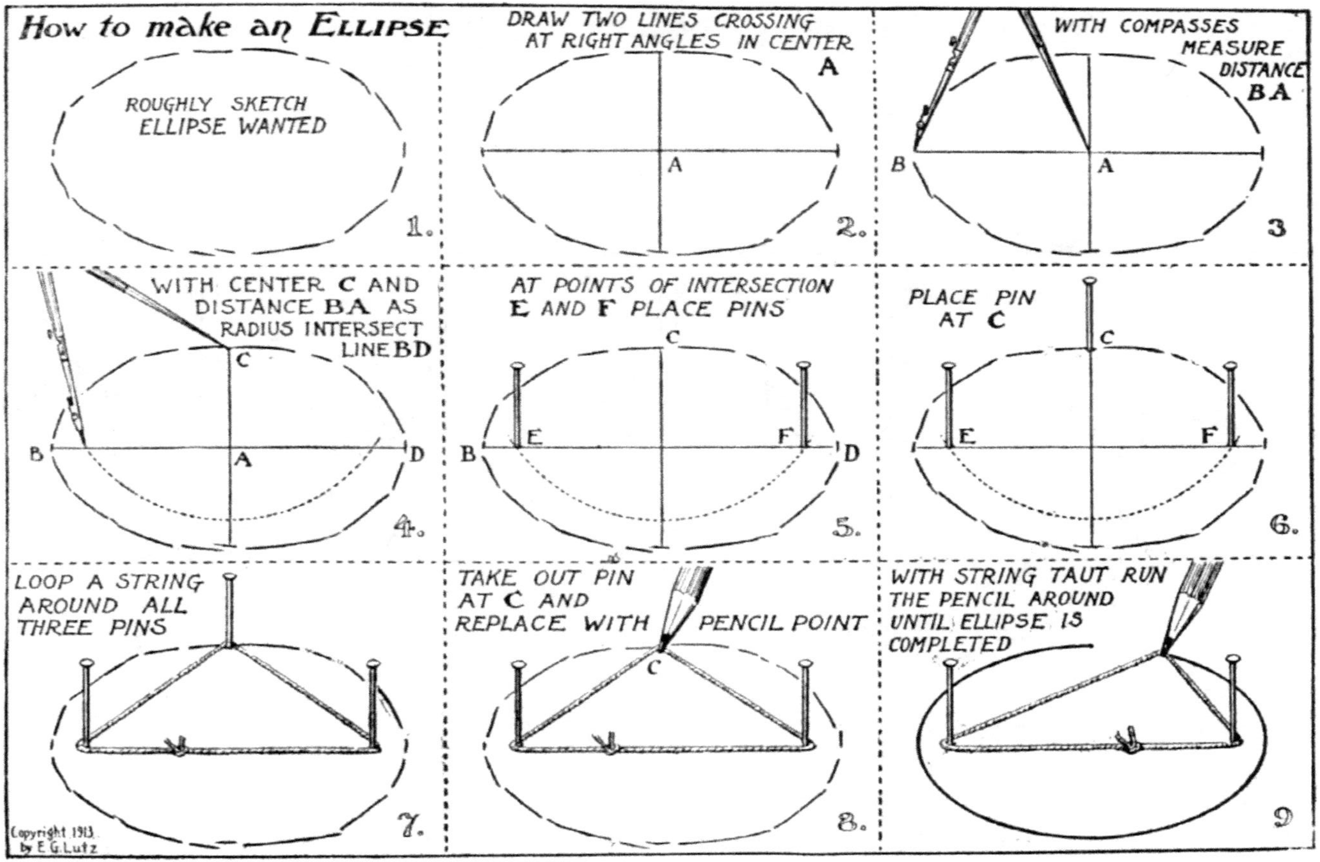
How to make an ELLIPSE
ROUGHLY SKETCH ELLIPSE WANTED
1.
DRAW TWO LINES CROSSING AT RIGHT ANGLES IN CENTER A
A
2.
WITH COMPASSES MEASURE DISTANCE BA
B
A
3
WITH CENTER C AND DISTANCE BA AS RADIUS INTERSECT LINE BD
C
B
A
D
4.
AT POINTS OF INTERSECTION E AND F PLACE PINS
C
E
F
B
D
5.
PLACE PIN AT C
C
E
F
6.
LOOP A STRING AROUND ALL THREE PINS
7.
TAKE OUT PIN AT C AND REPLACE WITH PENCIL POINT
C
8.
WITH STRING TAUT RUN THE PENCIL AROUND UNTIL ELLIPSE IS COMPLETED
9
Copyright 1913 by E. G. Lutz

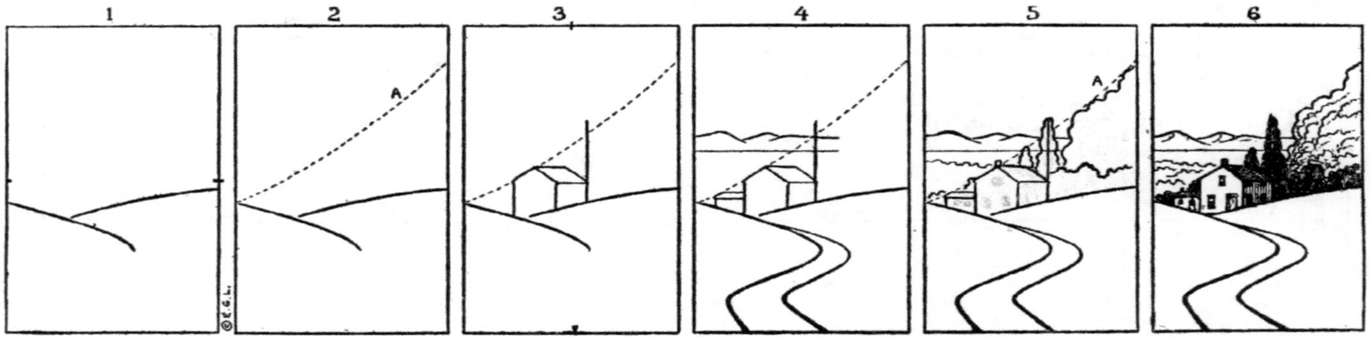
1
2
A
3
4
5
A
6
©E.G.L.

SUGGESTIONS FOR WATER-COLOR PAINTING

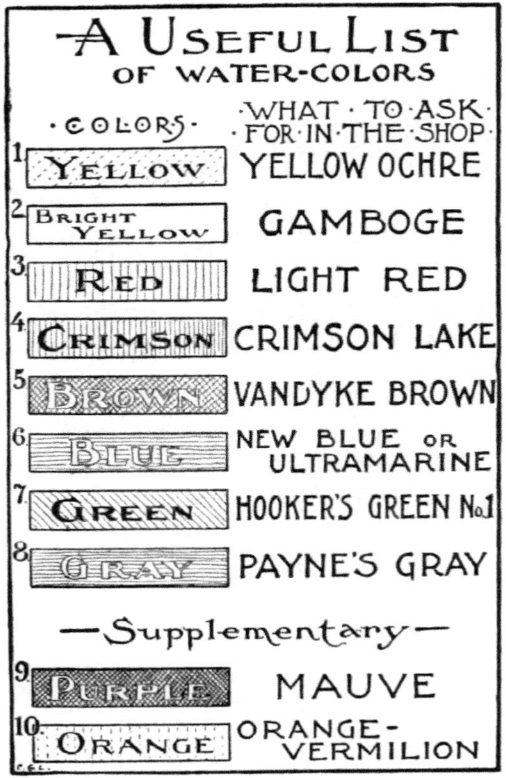
A USEFUL LIST
OF WATER-COLORS
·COLORS·
·WHAT·TO·ASK·
·FOR·IN·THE·SHOP·
1 YELLOW
YELLOW OCHRE
2 BRIGHT YELLOW
GAMBOGE
3 RED
LIGHT RED
4 CRIMSON
CRIMSON LAKE
5 BROWN
VANDYKE BROWN
6 BLUE
NEW BLUE OR ULTRAMARINE
7 GREEN
HOOKER'S GREEN No.1
8 GRAY
PAYNE'S GRAY
—Supplementary—
9 PURPLE
MAUVE
10 ORANGE
ORANGE-VERMILION

Here is a good list of colors for practical work. The first eight are enough for every purpose; but add, if you wish, purple and orange. Moist colors in pans are best. There are many different kinds of red, green, blue and brown paints; and as you may be puzzled and not know what to get, the names of the best hues of these particular colors are also given. The most useful paints in this list are yellow ochre, light red, Vandyke brown and Payne's gray. Learn to work with them, use them often and see the beautiful effects they produce. Delicate tints are made with thin washes of yellow ochre and light red. Vandyke brown makes a variety of pleasing tints.

Use the bright colors sparingly.

You do not need a black paint. Payne's gray with either brown, blue, crimson or green gives rich dark tones. Payne's gray is also useful in shadows and shading other colors. For the different kinds of greens, mix yellow ochre, blue or brown with Hooker's green. Use thin washes of light red and blue for the gray of distances and clouds.

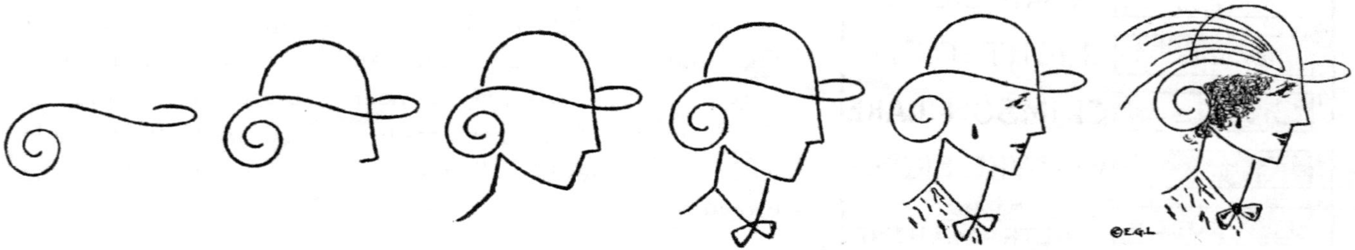
©E.G.L

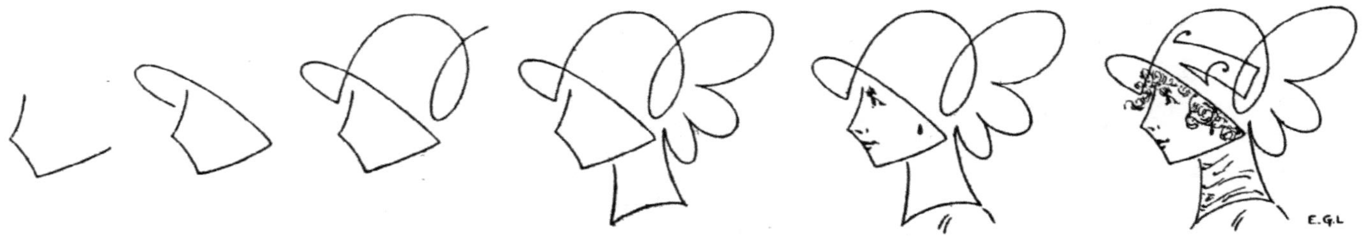
E.G.L

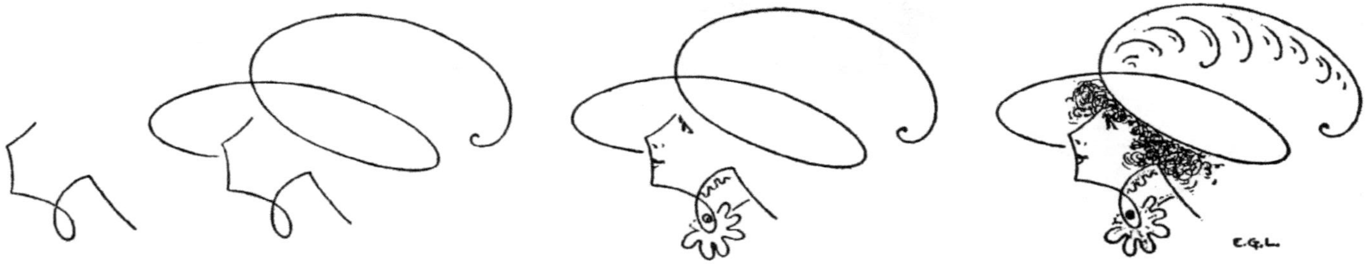
E.G.L.

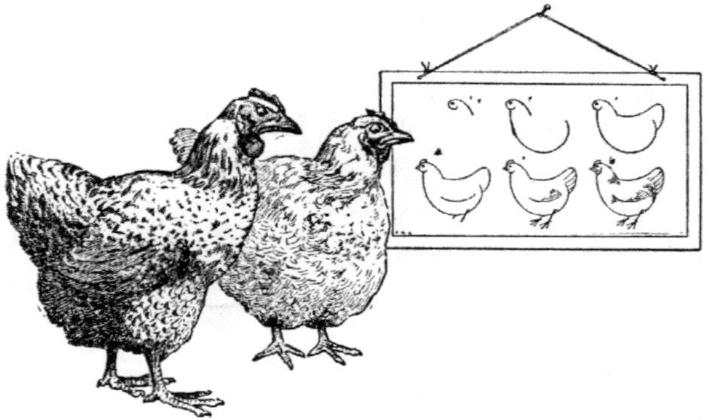

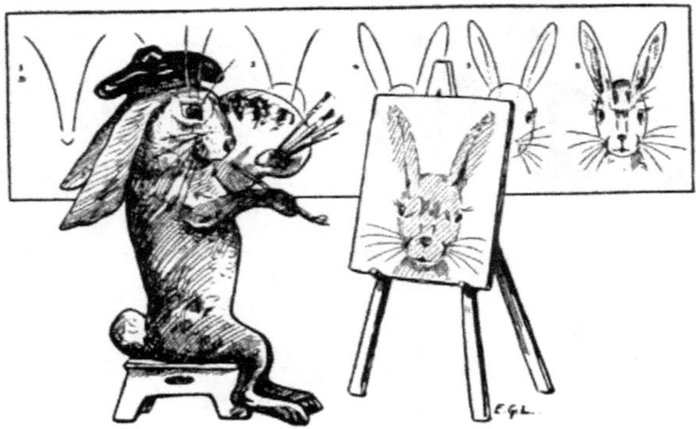
E.G.L.

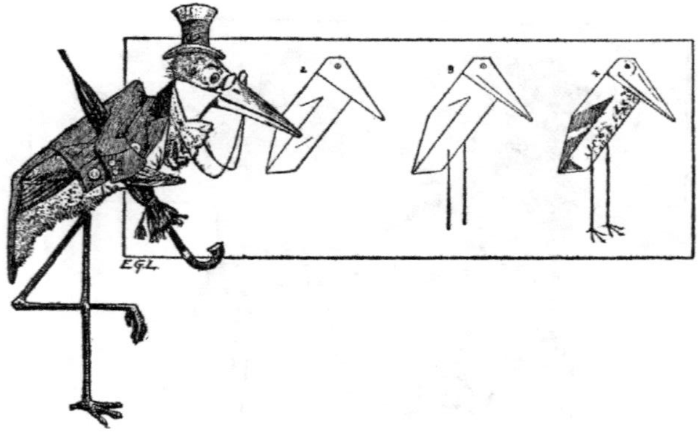
EGL

www.ingramcontent.com/pod-product-compliance
Lightning Source LLC
Chambersburg PA
CBHW051222170526
45166CB00005B/2000
* 9 7 8 1 5 1 9 6 1 5 5 1 0 *